C000146552

TRANSITION

Dave Harris

FOSTERING BETTER COLLABORATION BETWEEN
PRIMARY AND SECONDARY SCHOOLS

ındependent
thinking press

First published by

Independent Thinking Press
Crown Buildings, Bancyfelin, Carmarthen, Wales, SA33 5ND, UK
www.independentthinkingpress.com

and

Independent Thinking Press
PO Box 2223, Williston, VT 05495, USA
www.crownhousepublishing.com

Independent Thinking Press is an imprint of
Crown House Publishing Ltd.

Edited by Ian Gilbert.

The Independent Thinking On ... series is typeset in Azote, Buckwheat TC Sans,
Cormorant Garamond and Montserrat.

The Independent Thinking On ... series cover style was designed by Tania Willis
www.taniawillis.com.

British Library Cataloguing-in-Publication Data
A catalogue entry for this book is available from the British Library.

Print ISBN 978-178135340-0
Mobi ISBN 978-178135360-8
ePub ISBN 978-178135361-5
ePDF ISBN 978-178135362-2

LCCN 2019957447

Printed and bound in the UK by
Gomer Press, Llandysul, Ceredigion

FOREWORD

Since establishing Independent Thinking in 1994, we have worked hard to share with educators around the world our belief that there is always another way. The Independent Thinking On ... series of books is an extension of that work, giving a space for great educators to use their words and share great practice across a number of critical and relevant areas of education.

Independent Thinking on Transition addresses one of the biggest elephants in the room when it comes to seeking to raise achievement for all children in all of our schools. We have created a system that deliberately throws a massive bump in the road for children to navigate at a time when they are still young and vulnerable. Rather than helping them move smoothly through their educational childhood and into adolescence and young adulthood, we throw everything up in the air just at the point when they were starting to make sense of the world around them and their place within it.

Of course, many young people deal with this process like any other rite of passage – a challenge, possibly unpleasant, but just what you have to go through. After all, my parents did before me, and their parents before them.

But, as ever, there is another way.

Drawing on his experience in all sorts of schools in various parts of the world, including establishing a 3–18 all-through school in a former pit village in Nottinghamshire, Independent Thinking Associate Dave Harris shares insights, tips and ideas for primary and secondary schools, encouraging and inspiring them to work together to make the whole process of transition not just less of an ordeal but an altogether more positive and constructive event for all concerned.

A head teacher I met once described trying to get primary and secondary schools to work together on better transition practices as being like 'mating a cat and a dog'. With this book we can all come together to address the elephant, cat and dog, and create an altogether better animal for our young people.

IAN GILBERT
LINCOLN

ACKNOWLEDGEMENTS

I would like to thank the many wonderful teachers, both primary and secondary, who step out of their comfort zone to help give young people a stimulating educational journey.

Thank you to the inspiring team at Independent Thinking who continue to provide solutions in a world so often full of negativity and accountability. Thank you to Ian in particular for making it all happen.

Thank you to my wife, Esther, for her unstinting support and belief in me, and to my daughters, Beth and Meg, for their talents and passions and for reminding me why this is all so important.

CONTENTS

FIRST THOUGHTS

'We have a brilliant transition programme,' proudly claimed one secondary school leader I met recently. I held my breath in anticipation of finding the educational holy grail I had been searching for. 'We have two great days in early July when the primary kids visit us and do a forensic science project.'

My heart sank.

This is not brilliant transition. In fact, it probably isn't transition at all.

I have been working in the area of transition for over 15 years, creating one of England's first all-through 3–18 state schools in the early 2000s. Back at that time, I wrote a book called *Are You Dropping the Baton?*, which focused on ways of improving the transition from primary to secondary education.[1] In it, I painted a positive picture of what schools can achieve when they work closely together. However, it is with great sadness that I can see the gap has not narrowed over the past decade. Indeed, there are many signs indicating that it has in fact widened. We are now staring into not a gap but a chasm, one that claims more victims every year.

Surely, enough is now enough. The time for action is here. In this short book, my aim is to succinctly highlight the issues causing this problem, and then to offer some straightforward and practical solutions to remove them. The book is organised into four main sections: in Chapter 1 (The Chasm) we explore what the problem is and its effect

---

1   D. Harris, *Are You Dropping the Baton? From Effective Collaboration to All-Through Schools – Your Guide to Improving Transition* (Independent Thinking Series) (Carmarthen: Crown House Publishing, 2007).

on learning; in Chapter 2 (Bridging the Chasm) I propose a seven-step process to improve transition; in Chapter 3 (Success Factors) we consider other features that affect transition; and in the appendices there are materials to support the ideas put forward in the book.

The secondary school I mention on page 1 may have designed and executed a couple of fun days for their new pupils, and this is probably something worth doing. But if we believe it is solving the transition problem then we are fooling ourselves. At the very best, this type of event helps pupils to feel positive about their new school and enables them to become familiar with some new faces, names and rooms. However, it does nothing to develop coherent learning and progression, and in some cases it might even be construed as false marketing.

There can be a big difference between what a secondary school puts on during days like these and the diet of lessons served up once the children are on roll. I am not suggesting that fun learning events should be avoided, but we need to be clear that their role is simply about smoothing the bumps as young people deal with some of the many differences they will find between the two types of institution.

Let's get the language straight from the start. These types of event are not about *transition* but *induction* – inducting pupils into new places and procedures. Transition, on the other hand, needs to be a much longer, more detailed and ambitious process. Indeed, in its perfect form, transition begins on entry to primary school and finishes when the child leaves secondary school.[2] The following figure summarises the two approaches.

---

2   See D. Harris and J. West-Burnham, *Leadership Dialogues II: Leadership in Times of Change* (Carmarthen: Crown House Publishing, 2018), section 1D.

INDUCTION

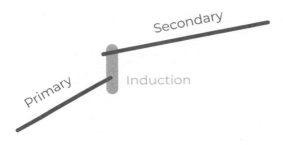

TRANSITION

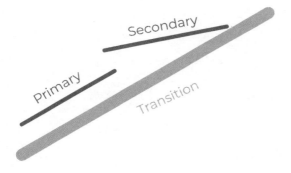

While evidence suggests that any change of school is a time when transition issues need to be addressed, for the purposes of this book I will focus on the issues experienced by pupils as they move between primary and secondary school.

CHAPTER 1

THE CHASM

Before I take you on a short history lesson of the education system to help you understand the thinking – or lack of it – behind the current system, let us first agree on what the outcomes of a successful transition process might be.

Back in 2008, the then Department for Children, Schools and Families produced a report on transition in which they defined the following key indicators of pupils enjoying a successful transition:

1 *Developing new friendships and improving self-esteem and confidence.*

2 *Settling so well in school life that parents have no concerns.*

3 *Showing an increasing interest in school and school work.*

4 *Getting used to new routines and school organisation with great ease.*

5 *Experiencing curriculum continuity.*[1]

Over a decade after this report was published, we would find it hard to disagree that a pupil exhibiting these traits has experienced a successful transition (although the phrase 'showing an increasing interest in school and

---

1   M. Evangelou, B. Taggart, K. Sylva, E. Melhuish, P. Sammons and I. Siraj-Blatchford, *What Makes a Successful Transition from Primary to Secondary School?* Research Report DCSF-RR019 (London: Department for Children, Schools and Families, 2008), pp. 53–54. Available at: https://dera.ioe.ac.uk/8618/1/DCSF-RR019.pdf.

school work' might have caused a few raised eyebrows in primary schools).

The basic needs of transition have probably not changed a great deal in 50 years, let alone 10. While the report suggested that a good number of pupils interviewed scored favourably on all five criteria, my own experiences would lead me to be less optimistic that we're getting it right. Most of the young people I encounter report few issues with items 1 and 4 (the areas on which many schools focus) but they are definitely not scoring high when it comes to areas 3 and 5. In a recent interview that I carried out with pupils one year after transition, under 30% thought that learning was more interesting than at their primary school.

I believe that the current focus on accreditation and testing in many parts of the world has driven secondary education into a traditional enclave where the test has become the goal rather than a tool in the process. To counter this, I would propose that the list on page 5 could be updated to include two more measures:

6 Understanding that education is more than just the exam grade achieved.

7 Understanding that you are never too old to enjoy learning.

How does your school measure up to these criteria today? What are you doing well? What could you improve? Where do you start?

According to a study by Marlau van Rens and colleagues, the most obvious but least used place to start is by asking young people themselves:

> *the involvement of children in decision-making by giving them a voice has been an area of growing interest … The*

absence of any direct consultation with the children involved in the transition process demonstrates the low priority given to this aspect of transfer. It should be possible for secondary schools to learn from children by asking incoming students about their thoughts about the transition, and ask recently switched students about their experiences and what they can suggest to smoothen the transition for other children.[2]

In England, at least, student voice has been forced into the backseat in recent years as 'teacher talk' has been given its place front and centre. But in transition, as in many other aspects of school life, we would do well to give children and young people a platform from which to speak about their experiences and a commitment that we will listen to them.

But how have things come to this? As is so often the case, in order to move forward more effectively, we need to look at the past.

A BRIEF HISTORY OF THE PRIMARY AND SECONDARY DIVIDE

As with all things education, let's start with the brain. After all, the more education is focused on the neuroscience of learning – the small electrical changes at the heart of all we do – the better we will be at designing an education system that is genuinely fit for purpose. With this in mind,

---

2   M. van Rens, C. Haelermans, W. Groot and H. Maassen van den Brink, Facilitating a Successful Transition to Secondary School: (How) Does it Work? A Systematic Literature Review, *Adolescent Research Review* 3(1) (2018): 43–56. Available at: https://link.springer.com/article/10.1007%2Fs40894-017-0063-2.

let's get something clear from the start: the traditional splitting of education into primary and secondary has absolutely nothing to do with the brain. It should do, but it doesn't. The historic reason for separating education into distinct phases is firmly rooted in practicalities.

In the past, education was a very local affair, often based in a single room close to the homes of its pupils. Children of all ages were taught in the same space, usually in lines, with the youngest at the front and the oldest at the back. Without becoming carried away by romantic reflections on the good old days of education, we can at least picture an educational environment focused, by necessity, on engagement, and not on the data-driven, achievement-focused system now seen in many parts of the world.

My own grandmother, a bright, intelligent woman, talked with passion about her time in her school in Neen Sollars, in rural England in the early 20th century. She described how the line between learner and teacher was frequently blurred, the pupils often learning as much from one another as they did from the teacher. General topics would be discussed by the whole class, then individual work would follow, with older children often supporting the learning of younger ones. Work was set at a variety of levels to support the different learning needs – differentiation before it had a name.

I was always impressed by her detailed knowledge of the geography of the world: she knew every country, capital city and major river, despite having never left her home in deepest Shropshire. She explained how, in her first weeks at school, she sat near the globe at the front of the class and, within days, an older pupil was enthusiastically sharing its hidden secrets. Each time a new pupil arrived at the school, the introduction was repeated and expanded, and her knowledge and interest increased. By the time she left the school she was leading the whole class in geography. These days we would call such an approach a 'spiral curriculum', in which learning is revisited regularly and expanded on each time (there is more on the spiral curriculum in Chapter 2).

This type of school is called a 'one-room school' and, although there are many rural communities where such schooling still exists, in general it is an approach that has disappeared from the educational landscape in many parts of the world. As transport improved, larger schools were possible, and following the principles of a burgeoning industrial society, larger was seen as more efficient. Bigger schools meant that the model of teaching all the children together was growing increasingly untenable, and so a method was needed to separate them into different classes.

The obvious way to achieve this was by age, which also helped to moderate noise levels for the older pupils, allowed for the introduction of smaller furniture for smaller children and provided the opportunity for a very different curriculum for the youngest pupils. As workforce requirements broadened through the Industrial Revolution and the growth of the British Empire, the need to provide a wider 'specialist' curriculum grew. Housing all of this provision under one roof often proved impractical, and so different sites for different ages developed. These are the seeds from which grew two separate organisms – the primary and secondary schools with which we are now familiar.

It is a law of nature that when systems grow in isolation from each other, it is almost inevitable that they will develop different approaches, attitudes and beliefs. This is certainly true of primary and secondary education. In many places they have evolved separately for over 100 years with little regard to the needs of young people.

The situation is further exacerbated by the argument that primary-age children learn best in one way and secondary pupils learn best in a different way. Too often these assumptions have little basis in the facts. Of course, the brain of a 3-year-old and an 18-year-old have different levels of maturity and will respond in different ways to stimulation, but the neuroscience of learning suggests that the variations between the two are not as great as our school systems would suggest.

I asked paediatric neurologist and Independent Thinking Associate Dr Andrew Curran for his opinion. Does the brain suddenly change to learn in a different way at the age of 11? From a neurological perspective, is a sharp transition between two very different environments the best way to learn?

He was very clear. The brain does not suddenly undergo a transformation at a set age. First, brain development happens at different rates for every child. Ideally, any alterations in the environment to accommodate changes in the process of learning should be done as needed and not at some arbitrary age. Second, while many changes happen to the brain between infancy and adulthood, they all require a gradual change in environment, not an abrupt one. In fact, viewed from a neurological perspective, the 'jolt' experienced by young people as they pass from primary to secondary school could hardly happen at a worse time – and, for many, it is an experience from which they never recover.

ARE ALL-THROUGH SCHOOLS THE ANSWER?

The answer to this question is very much 'it depends'. I am passionate about all-through schooling, having been something of a trendsetter by bringing together what had been three separate schools – infant, junior and secondary – in a former pit village in Nottinghamshire. Furthermore, I have visited numerous all-age schools around the world, many of which have impressed me with their vision and practice when it comes to getting transition right. But there have also been too many that saddened me. These schools seemed to think that the only reason for having all the phases on one site was to make it easier for parents. Rather than using their geography to improve transition, these schools often perpetuated the barriers between the ages, failing to make the most of their opportunity to pro-duce a smooth learning journey for their pupils.

One school visit encapsulated my frustrations with the way the different phases can fail to work together in a complementary way. As usual, I began my tour with the youngest pupils and walked through the school in chronological order, finishing with the oldest learners. The infant classes were a joy to behold. I saw motivated, happy children working at their own pace, sometimes on their own and sometimes in groups. I saw pupil–teacher co-construction of learning, with the infants deciding with their teacher what tasks they would do and in what order, and even peer assessment as the children helped each other to improve their work. Such practices filled me with hope for the development of high-quality, independent learners across the school, and I could barely contain my excitement as I anticipated what I would see next.

Sadly, rather than the infant section being the start of a wonderful journey, it proved to be the beginning of a tragedy. As I walked through the school, I observed that early enthusiasm replaced with tedium: the older the pupils, the more sedentary and passive they became. I saw less group work as the learners' age increased, and I saw little or no evidence of co-construction or peer assessment. The typical classroom contained a teacher at the front talking. Most of the older pupils seemed disinterested in their work (with a handful appearing to be asleep!). The palpable excitement for learning I had found among the infants was replaced by boredom in the oldest pupils. My frustration was compounded when I asked the head teacher what her aims were for the school. She quickly replied that it was to produce 'happy, motivated, independent learners'. Really?! That was what the children had started with, yet the school seemed to be systematically driving out that happiness, motivation and independence.

I am a scientist by training, so I began to investigate how one school could contain such wildly different approaches to teaching and learning. I interviewed the infant teachers who were, in my opinion, some of the most talented and imaginative teachers I had ever observed. Their passion for the type of active learning they had developed was intense. I asked them how often they were able to share their work with the teachers of older pupils in the school, and the answer was a sad but almost inevitable 'never'. They were not even allowed to use the same staffroom as the other teachers, making them feel as if they were not 'real' teachers, and they were not invited to whole-school staff meetings, let alone being asked to lead them.

This is an important early message: co-location of schools does not always lead to improved transition. Indeed, the all-through school I established had schools split across three sites in the town. A school is more than a building; a philosophical closeness is much more important than a geographical one.

IS IT REALLY THAT BAD – AFTER ALL, SOME YOUNG PEOPLE ACHIEVE SUCCESS?

I have often heard people (and not just politicians) protest that the current system can't be that bad because they – or someone they know – did OK. They might point out that they genuinely enjoyed the abrupt process of transition and found the sudden change of school to be beneficial. I suggest that this is akin to arguing that smoking isn't bad for your health because Great Aunt Maud lived to be 100 and smoked 20 cigarettes a day.

Put simply, transition should not be about survival; it should be about engaging in an exciting new phase of learning.[3]

Most of us have grown up with a change of school around the onset of adolescence. 'When are you off to big school?' is a standard question we are asked. It is part of our culture, so perhaps we accept this as a rite of passage and a normal part of growing up. But maybe we need to look beyond this tradition and ask ourselves whether it really makes sense.

---

3   That said, recent research shows that physically active children tend to deal better with transition than their more sedentary peers, so maybe there is an element to transition of survival of the fittest after all: E. A. Haapala, H. L. Haapala, H. Syvaoja, T. H. Tammelin, T. Finni and N. Kiuru, Longitudinal Associations of Physical Activity and Pubertal Development with Academic Achievement in Adolescents, *Journal of Sport and Health Science* (2019). https://doi.org/10.1016/j.jshs.2019.07.003.

Imagine a world where the same approach is made in family life. A world where, on the morning of a child's eleventh birthday, he or she is expected to move to a new family on the other side of town. 'We've enjoyed being your first family, darling. Good luck in your new home – hope you settle in quickly. And do come back and visit us, won't you!' Madness, and yet this is our preferred method for schooling.

What is surprising about this is that over the years many studies have emerged with the same message: transition from primary to secondary school is causing damage to many children. And there is plenty of evidence of a dip in both educational achievement and the well-being of some pupils.

For example, researchers from the University of Dundee carried out an international review of research in this area. They investigated over 4,500 records, including 14 in-depth studies in the UK and United States. While there were obviously differences between the findings, some common threads also came to light. With regard to educational attainment, the report's authors highlight:

- *All 14 studies that focussed on educational outcomes provided fairly robust evidence that there was a decline in pupils' educational outcomes after they moved to secondary school.*

- *Eight of these studies used either examination scores or standardised test scores to provide evidence of decline in grades achieved by the pupils after the transition to secondary school, with three providing evidence of a decline over a number of years ... However, whether this decline was as a direct result of the transition to secondary school is less clear ...*

- *Some studies reported declines in motivation, school engagement and attitudes towards some subjects, and increase in absence and dropping out. These could potentially explain the reasons for decline in grades, or vice versa.*[4]

With regard to the impact on the well-being of pupils, the authors noted the following:

- *A small number of studies found either no negative outcomes or some positive outcomes for a small number of pupils ...*

- *Other studies found negative impact of transitions on wellbeing including increase in school misbehaviour, decline in feelings of school belongingness and connectedness, poorer social and emotional health, and higher levels of depression and anxiety.*

- *Increase in pupils' anxiety during transitions was associated with decreased connectedness to school and decline in perceived school belongingness over time.*[5]

There is certainly a problem, and the vital issue of belonging is right at the heart of it.

Shamila Vaz and colleagues set out to investigate the concept of belongingness – how much a pupil feels they belong in a specific school environment. In particular, they considered how the level of belongingness affects the success of transition. Their conclusions are unsurprising:

Findings of the present study offer an empirical foundation for the need for school-based initiatives aimed at increasing

---

4   D. Jindal-Snape, D. Cantali, S. MacGillivray and E. Hannah, *Primary to Secondary School Transitions: Systematic Literature Review* (Edinburgh: Scottish Government, 2019), p. 14. Available at: https://www.gov.scot/publications/primary-secondary-transitions-systematic-literature-review/pages/2.

5   Jindal-Snape et al., *Primary to Secondary School Transitions*, p. 15.

belongingness in secondary school. The literature suggests that among youth in transition, those who are able to develop a better sense of belonging in school are more likely to have better outcomes, both in school and beyond.[6]

This gives weight to the idea that any process which helps to increase familiarity and engenders a sense of belonging will produce a more successful transition.

It is clearly the case that some young people quickly come to feel that they belong in the new school, dealing with the process of transition well enough to continue on to great success. Perhaps a combination of home life and peer support is at play here too, but transition quickly vanishes as an issue for them. For other students, however, it is the start of a disconnect in their schooling from which they never fully recover.

While most observers do not dispute the existence of these two types of experience, the relative percentage of pupils in each group is a moot point. Teachers have given me estimates ranging from 10–35% for pupils who have experienced a long-term negative effect. However, if you consider how many children make the transition from primary to secondary each year, even if the number affected is at the low end of the predictions, this is still a very serious problem and one that we must resolve.

---

6   S. Vaz, M. Falkmer, M. Ciccarelli and A. E. Passmore, Belongingness in Early Secondary School: Key Factors that Primary and Secondary Schools Need to Consider, *PLoS ONE* 10(9) (2015): e0136053.

WHY MIGHT PROBLEMS OCCUR WITH TRANSITION?

As I have described briefly a little earlier in this chapter, the primary and secondary phases of education have been allowed to develop in isolation – which has resulted in some stark differences.

The list below is not meant to be emotive – do try to read it without letting your hackles rise! The differences are not meant as a judgement but simply as an observation of what is typical in most schools. Nearly all the primary and secondary teachers I have met simply want to do an amazing job and have excellent relationships with their pupils. That is not in question. What we are looking at here are the limitations placed on those relationships.

- **Buildings**
  - ▲ *Primary*: Often cosy, with a family feel.
  - ▲ *Secondary*: Often large and impressive, with the 'wow factor' evident in many new builds.

- **Decor**
  - ▲ *Primary*: Bright, colourful, often pupil generated and celebratory in nature.
  - ▲ *Secondary*: Displays are often commercially produced and examination focused.

- **Arrival in school**
  - ▲ *Primary*: Parents often accompany their children into school and help add to the 'family feel' that pervades. Teachers are often around to welcome pupils, often led from the front by the head teacher. The tone for the day is set: this is a safe and happy place where we all enjoy learning.

▲ *Secondary:* Parents are generally not encouraged into school, at least not without an appointment. The primary initial interaction with staff is often around checking uniform and procedures. The tone for the day is set: the adults are in control and will ensure that pupils are engaging in their core learning.

● **Lessons**

▲ *Primary:* Most lessons are taught by one teacher. In general, when there is a change in teacher, the teacher comes to the pupils, who remain in their own classroom.

▲ *Secondary:* Pupils have between five and eight different lessons each day, most occurring in separate parts of the school.

● **Learning**

▲ *Primary:* Interconnected learning is common, with more than one topic being covered in the same piece of work. Group work and project work are familiar methods of delivery and the co-construction of learning (pupils helping to design their own learning) is also a regular occurrence.

▲ *Secondary:* Lessons are usually individual affairs, and usually linked to previous learning in that subject rather than to learning in other subjects. Classrooms are frequently more teaching oriented, with the focus being on delivering the syllabus.

● **Trust**

▲ *Primary:* Pupils are often given responsibility from an early age. The older pupils in the school may be given important whole-school tasks and trusted in a variety of ways.

▲ *Secondary*: The oldest pupils are sometimes given important roles, but younger ones are often afforded little or no trust. When pupils do have the teachers' trust, it tends to be earned rather than given.

These differences have a cumulative effect, adding up to create an atmosphere specific to each phase. It is not about one necessarily being better than the other, it is just different. I have visited many wonderful schools over the past decade, but I could usually identify the age of the pupils from the 'feel' of the building. Of course, some changes become necessary as a result of raging hormones and the needs of older pupils, but many are just a by-product of the two systems developing in isolation.

The reflections above are based on my own experiences from many years spent in schools in the UK and worldwide. Jane Tobbell provides a more academic perspective on the transition between two 'typical' schools in the table on pages 20–21.[7] While no attempt is made to suggest that these findings are true for every transition, the table provides a checklist against which to compare your own situation.

Consider my list and the list from Tobbell's research on pages 20–21. How does your school compare? Do you recognise your school in either or both lists? Are you happy with that? If you could, would you make any changes? Perhaps there is another way?

To further highlight the illogical nature of the transition process – and throw up some interesting perspectives and questions that we might not have thought of before – let's

7   J. Tobbell, Transition from Primary to Secondary School: A Case Study from the United Kingdom. In A. B. Liegmann, I. Mammes and K. Racherbaumer (eds), *Facetten von Übergangen im Bildungssystem: Nationale und internationale Ergebnisse empirischer Forschung* (Münster: Waxmann, 2014), pp. 251-264 at pp. 260-261.

Primary X	Secondary Y
Physical space	**Physical space**
• Each class has a dedicated classroom.	• The students meet in a tutor group room at the beginning and end of each day.
• Each child has personal desk space.	• The students move rooms every lesson. They do not enter classrooms until they are invited by the teacher and are expected to form an orderly queue outside the class.
• Each child has a space to hang their coat and bag.	
• The children stay in their classroom for most lessons.	• The students carry their coats and bags around with them; there is no space for their belongings.
• There is a playground where activities are provided for the children and supervised by adults.	• At break times students hang round the school grounds. Teachers are stationed at entrances to prevent access.
• The school houses 400 pupils and 21 teachers.	• The school houses over 1,000 pupils and over 100 staff members.

Teaching and learning	Teaching and learning
• 40% of time is taken up with study of maths, English and science.	• The day is divided into six separate lessons determined by a timetable. End of lessons is signified by a bell.
• The remainder of the time is devoted to religious education, history, geography, art and design, information technology, PE.	• The students have maths and English lessons five times per week.
• Teachers are generalists, trained as primary school teachers.	• The rest of the lessons are divided equally between the remaining subjects, which include two foreign languages, design and technology, music, history, geography, PE, combined science, personal and social development, religious education.
• One or two teachers lead the class for all topics.	
• The teacher determines the amount of time spent on a subject, which varies.	• Teachers have undergraduate degrees in their specific subjects and are trained to teach those subjects.
• Study is often topic based – for example, a class might study the Egyptians, which involves history, geography, IT, religion and art and music.	• Each lesson tends to follow the same format.
• The pace of the day is determined by the teacher and is divided into whole class, group and individual activities.	• The teacher presents the subject material and the class engages in individual activity.
• Children are expected to have a book to read and time is devoted to this at registration and at the end of activities.	• The lessons are structured by a textbook.

compare two very different education systems. In recent years, I have worked extensively in both England and Slovenia, countries that usually appear in the top 20 PISA rankings, but which arrange their schooling in very different ways:

Phase	England	Slovenia
Primary	5–11-year-olds	6–15-year-olds
Secondary	11–16 (or 18)-year-olds	15–18-year-olds

Having spent time in schools in both countries, what becomes evident is that there are issues around transition in both systems. However, the different ages at which this occurs emphasises that the problems are *not* related to pupils' ages but more to the nature of system change.

For example, some stark differences emerge when observing 12-year-olds in both systems. The style of education experienced by English 12-year-olds tends to be more formal and examination based, while the Slovenian system maintains a more primary feel with more cross-curricular and project-focused lessons.

The following comparison may seem a trivial example, but I believe it exemplifies the difference in approach I have observed. The first photo shows the door to a typical maths room used by 12-year-old pupils in England:

And this is a maths room door used by 12-year-olds in a school in Grosuplje, Slovenia:

This simple illustration typifies an unwritten rule that seems to have been adopted by many – if not most – countries in the developed world: *primary school is fun, and secondary school – big school – is serious.*

This really worries me.

Of course, as a child approaches adulthood we want them to become more focused on their future and to see the importance of their studies. But just because the stakes are higher, does that mean we have to make the learning more serious? After all, as we have been known to say at Independent Thinking, learning is too important to be taken seriously.

Going back to the brain, neuroscientists consistently report that the adult brain is not fully formed until an individual is in their mid-twenties. The idea that a teenager's brain will respond in the same way as an adult's brain is clearly nonsensical. What may seem logical to a 30-year-old may not make sense to a 13-year-old. In fact, the teenage brain is a complex soup of chemicals and neural connections – a curious process known as 'hairy dendritic sprouting'.

Furthermore, an adolescent's brain reward system is triggered in a different way to an adult's – for example, they have an approach to risk which would horrify most adults. I asked Dr Andrew Curran why it is that humans have been so badly designed – why the most vulnerable (i.e. young adults) have such a propensity for risk-taking and challenge. He replied that it was probably the single biggest positive factor in the survival of our species. Ensuring that young people do things differently to the generation before them, challenging rules and taking risks, means that as a species we develop and progress. So, the next time a teenager causes you grief, take some comfort from the fact that their behaviour is an indication of our species adapting to survive.

All this means that the drive to systematise learning – to make it routine and functionary and built around biological rather than neurological age – is not necessarily going to benefit the typical teenager.[8]

It is important to stress that I am not pointing an accusatory finger at the teaching profession, but rather at the politicians and those in the media who try to perpetuate a flawed system based on questionable practices from a century ago. In many parts of the world we have allowed some simple stereotypes to become true, encouraging the population to believe that the function of schooling is to produce better and better exam results rather than develop young people who enjoy learning.

Too often in secondary schools (and some primary ones) I encounter teachers who believe their role is to deliver a dense curriculum and that their success is dependent on them 'covering' the 150 learning points in the syllabus. It saddens me when I hear teachers say, 'I would love to try the active learning you're talking about, Dave, but I just don't have the time. I only have 30 lessons before the exam and X syllabus points still to teach them!' The evidence seems to point to the fact that the well-known maxim that education is not the filling of a pail but the lighting of a fire is still not really believed by many in the teaching profession. The focus on curriculum delivery has strangled the pleasure out of learning for many pupils (and their teachers).

---

8   A challenging thought here is that there is little evidence to suggest that even a fully mature adult brain learns best in formal, sterile surroundings. Most participants I meet at teacher conferences and INSET days say that they learn better when the learning is dynamic, engaging and delivered with an element of humour.

I recently had a very interesting conversation with a 14-year-old at the back of an English language class. This was a lower set group and he was clearly not the class angel. I asked him about the subject and his teacher. He sighed, leaned back in his chair and shook his head gently: 'Oh, the teacher is great, she really cares about us and does a top job. But what we're learning is a load of rubbish [he may have used a more colloquial alternative!]. The stuff she has to teach us is what my mum had to do 30 years ago. The curriculum is so out of date – I need something that will help me now!'

Out of the mouths of babes ...

CHAPTER 2

BRIDGING THE CHASM

It is my view – and the conclusion of many commentators on the subject – that having such a large gap between the two phases of education cannot be a good thing for the children going through it.[1] So, we recognise there is a problem; although some may disagree with me on its importance, there is a problem.

Let's now turn our attention to how we can begin to rethink the process of transition in order to ensure a more cohesive approach to education – one that will benefit all children and young people.

I am proposing a seven-step approach to transition to help us in this goal. It is an approach born out of experience and empirical observation, and it is meant to be straightforward and achievable, wherever there is the will to make the necessary changes.

The seven steps are as follows:

1   Agree on the long-term aims of education in your geographical area.

2   Improve teacher understanding of each phase.

3   Improve pupil understanding of the long-term goals of their education.

---

1   I have met the occasional diehard traditionalist who has voiced the idea that completely separating primary and secondary is desirable, enabling, in their words, 'Secondary school to have the shock, awe and wonder effect.' I suggest that, as with any such claim, we always need to add the caveat question: at what cost?

4   Encourage opportunities for pupils of different ages and phases to learn together.

5   Develop a curriculum plan from infant to adult for your geographical area.

6   Build learning experiences between the phases into the calendar.

7   Make sure your induction programme is a subset of your transition programme.

I will now take you through the steps in turn and then suggest examples of the types of practice that I have either delivered or seen in action that will help to set the ball rolling.

STEP 1: AGREE ON THE LONG-TERM AIMS OF EDUCATION IN YOUR GEOGRAPHICAL AREA

Coming to an agreement on the long-term aims of education may seem like a big ask as the first step, especially if community-based local authority and governance has been eroded and replaced with a more corporate approach to school management, as it has in England and the United States. But without addressing this important step transition will always be problematic.

I'm always one for a simple allegory, so let's imagine two families setting off on a joint camping holiday. Each family decides to travel in their own car, which means that agreeing the destination and intended arrival time becomes an essential part of the planning process. Without agreed goals there is every chance of a mismatch of both time and place.

If this logic is easy to apply for something as simple as a holiday, then surely it must be relevant for a complex journey such as education. This means that 'Where are we going?' is a vital question – or, couched in stronger but more controversial terms, 'What is education for?'

As outlined in both *Leadership Dialogues* books, which I co-wrote with Professor John West-Burnham, there is real cohesion among all the research that an essential ingredient of great leadership is clarity of vision.[2] Leaders are most effective when they help others to understand their purpose and goals, and this is as true in individual schools as it is across larger geographical areas. One test of a successful school is to ask the question, 'What is *this* school about?' to people from all roles within the establishment – the teachers, the leaders, the pupils, the parents, the premises staff, everyone. The closer the match between their answers, the increased likelihood that the school is successful.

So, the very first step for a school wishing to improve transition is to put its own vision under a microscope. What does your school website/prospectus say about your vision? Do staff, pupils and parents agree that this is exemplified in practice? If a visitor were to describe their perception of your school vision from a visit, would it match what you think your vision is? Remember, the genuine and authentic vision of a school is reflected by what it does, not by what it says it does.

Once you have examined your own vision, next up is to repeat the process with the other schools which form part of the transition arrangements in your area.

---

2   J. West-Burnham and D. Harris, *Leadership Dialogues: Conversations and Activities for Leadership Teams* (Carmarthen: Crown House Publishing, 2014); Harris and West-Burnham, *Leadership Dialogues II*.

THE VISION/NO-VISION MATRIX

		Primary school	
		Clear vision	Unclear vision
Secondary school	Clear vision	Scenario 1: Harmony or combat	Scenario 2: Help or hindrance
	Unclear vision	Scenario 3: Hindrance or help	Scenario 4: Discovering together

In my experience, this is when we start to see problems. Some schools have a crystal-clear vision, and others, well, not so much. Mathematically speaking, this leads to several possible combinations of what we might call the vision/no-vision matrix (see page 30). Each permutation needs a different approach, and some combinations are simpler to work with than others.[3]

SCENARIO 1: HARMONY OR COMBAT

Both schools in the transition partnership have a clear vision.

If both schools have a clearly stated vision which is echoed in day-to-day practice, this can be the perfect start to improving all aspects of the transition process. Then again, it could be a big problem.

Let me explain. If the two visions are broadly similar, then this offers the opportunity for both schools to come together around a single clear vision. Staff, pupils and parents will find working with the partner school non-threatening and exciting, and will understand the reason for future collaborations. Often, when staff from different phases work together the focus soon becomes the differences between the two philosophies, but when the visions converge any learning partnership is likely to be deep and long lasting.

However, if the two visions are well-defined, strong and acted on, but obviously quite different from each other,

---

3   Please note that, for simplicity, I am describing the relationship between a primary school and a secondary school. Many secondary schools have multiple feeder schools and many primary schools send children to multiple secondary schools, so the work to be done grows exponentially, but the same principles still apply.

the relationship between the two schools is far more likely to be problematic.

For example, if a primary school has a values-based philosophy and regards the identification, understanding and practice of values as their most important role, and the secondary school has a philosophy that achievement (measured in academic results) is the key to a pupil's long-term success, then the likelihood of a seamless transition is immediately greatly reduced.

Both perspectives may work very well for the individual schools, but they are not necessarily transferable between the two institutions. In this situation, the worst option is for both schools to ignore their differences and just soldier on, hoping it won't matter. This will not produce a smooth and effective learning journey for their pupils.

The ideal solution in this scenario is for both schools to try to find a new iteration of their vision which somehow bridges the differences between the two schools. For example, in the situation above, both schools could choose to work with a vision that ties values-based learning to achievement, clearly stating that doing your very best in all endeavours is a value shared by both institutions and is expected of all pupils (and teachers).

However, if either school digs in their heels and presents their vision as non-negotiable, this relationship is always likely to be difficult and transition is unlikely to be as effective as it could be.

SCENARIOS 2 AND 3: HELP OR HINDRANCE/HINDRANCE OR HELP

One of the schools – the primary or the secondary – involved in transition has a very clear vision which is clearly embedded in their everyday practice. The other school does not.

Interestingly, the same rules apply here as in the first scenario. This can be either a very productive collaboration or a disaster waiting to happen. It all depends on how palatable the clear vision of one school is to the other school. And, experience tells me that if it is the primary school with the clear vision, and not the secondary, then this complicates matters further.

That said, this relationship can be successful if the school without the clear vision fully agrees with the vision of the partner school. This can lead to a harmonious situation which is summed up neatly in the old nursery rhyme:

> *Jack Sprat could eat no fat.*
>
> *His wife could eat no lean.*
>
> *And so between them both, you see,*
>
> *They licked the platter clean.*

In other words, it is a relationship of convenience: we don't have a vision, so please can we share yours?

While the simplicity of this situation may appeal, it is fraught with danger. This will only work if the vision described and acted on by one school is categorically a perfect fit for the other school; indeed, is the very vision it has been looking for all this time. Even then, in such an unusual scenario, there is every likelihood that the balance of power will lie with the school whose vision has been adopted.

Let's be crystal clear here: the key to quality transition is a partnership of equals; equals who happen to teach different ages, but professional equals nonetheless.

If one school adopts the vision of the other there is every chance that it won't actually be a perfect fit. Remember that a vision is not what is written down on paper but the day-to-day experiences of those within the institution. Put simply, it is 'how things are done around here'. The practices that have developed in a school over the years are very unlikely to simply slot into an off-the-shelf vision from the school down the road – a fact that is not lost on academy groups trying to bring disparate schools together under one umbrella.[4]

If two schools find themselves in the second scenario, a strategy more likely to succeed would be for both to investigate whether a new area-wide vision can be found. Using the mission statement of the school with the clear and strong vision as a starting point, teams from both schools could meet with the first step to consider what the agreed aims for education in the area should be. Why do both schools exist? What do both schools consider as success?

These may be difficult questions to answer, so a useful technique to help get the conversation flowing is to find a photograph of the youngest learner from the primary school and one of the oldest pupils from the secondary school. Place these two photos side by side and ask the question, 'What do we want our youngest pupil to gain from their 12 years of learning with us?' This will focus the conversation on the reality of the matter rather than the theory.

---

4   'Please stop saying, "The people from the Trust are visiting today!" You *are* the Trust! We are *all* the Trust!' as I heard one increasingly hysterical Trust CEO telling a group of geographically diverse primary schools recently.

Once you have produced a list of the desired outcomes for your area's education system, the existing values statement should be considered in this light: 'If we were to deliver the stated vision in every part of the local system, would we get the outcomes we require? If not, how should the vision be reworked?'

For example, the group might produce a set of desired outcomes along these lines:

What we want for our learners when they leave our schools:

- To have good evaluation skills.
- To be able to communicate effectively in a variety of forms.
- To have a positive mindset.
- To be resilient.
- To enjoy their learning.
- To have good interpersonal skills.
- To get a range of qualifications to support their future.

The pre-existing vision statement might say something like:

Our vision is to develop young people with active and creative minds, a sense of understanding and compassion for others, and the courage to act on their beliefs. We stress the total development of each child: spiritual, moral, intellectual, social, emotional and physical.

This statement should then be dissected, not because it is wrong but in order to ascertain whether these laudable aims would produce everything that has been identified in the desired outcomes document. In this example, it could be argued the statement does not specifically address the stated desire to produce learners who are happy. Therefore the statement could be reworked to correct this shortcoming.[5]

Once a new vision statement has been developed, it is essential that it is not seen as a criticism of the old one, but instead as a positive next step or natural progression. The implications for the day-to-day life of the schools in question need to be considered too. What needs to be done to make this vision live? What will that look like in classrooms, corridors and staffrooms?

SCENARIO 4: DISCOVERING TOGETHER

This scenario may seem the least likely to succeed, but in fact it has great potential for success. With both schools coming into the relationship without a clearly stated and lived vision, there is the possibility of using the process of transition to bring everyone from the geographical area together around a new single vision for education. A new mission statement grown from the needs of the pupils

---

5   And by 'reworked' I don't mean just 'add it to the list'. After all, a vision is something that all members of an organisation should be able to carry around in their head.

could – and should – lead to a very powerful transition process.

The best first step here is for the schools to begin with the process described in scenarios 2 and 3, by agreeing on the desired outcomes for a learner who is just starting their education journey in your schools. If you have done a great job for this child, in what ways will they have benefitted?

This activity should be afforded plenty of time. It should not be seen as a trivial starter to an INSET day, for example, but as the key to producing a successful educational partnership in the area. Initially, don't attempt to do this as one big group, and instead encourage a 1-2-4-8-all approach. For example, ask individuals to attempt the task on their own first, then work with a pair to produce a composite, then two pairs and so on, until the group list reflects the thinking of everyone in the room.

Once this list has been produced it should be displayed in the staffrooms of all the schools, shared with governors, parents, pupils and anyone else with a stake in local education. It should not be presented as a finished item; additions and tweaks should be encouraged.

Once the intended outcomes of the educational journey have been agreed, an important question needs to be asked: how do we make this happen in practice? In other words, what do we need to do to make sure this is genuinely and palpably what schools are about? Your answers will lead to a set of desired actions, but before you dive headlong into making the vision a reality there is a useful check you can undertake.

Set the challenge of capturing your vision in the least number of words possible. Once an initial draft has been approved it should be displayed in each school alongside the agreed outcomes, with the question put to all members of the school community: 'If we fully live the vision outlined here, will these outcomes be produced? If not, what changes to the statement do we need?' A joint area vision for education produced in this way gives the best possible foundation for a long and successful transition relationship.

If anyone remains unconvinced that all of this is necessary, ask the next five adults you meet in your school, 'What is the purpose of education?' I predict that you will find yourself with five very different – and not always compatible – answers. If the adults are unclear of the goals of education, it isn't surprising that many children remain confused about why they are going through the process every day.

What's more, this is not a new phenomenon. Back in 1947, Dr Martin Luther King, Jr. wrote an item for the Morehouse College student newspaper under the heading 'The Purpose of Education'. In it he declared:

> *To save man from the morass of propaganda, in my opinion, is one of the chief aims of education. Education must enable one to sift and weigh evidence, to discern the true from the false, the real from the unreal, and the facts from the fiction.*
>
> *The function of education, therefore, is to teach one to think intensively and to think critically. But education which stops with efficiency may prove the greatest menace to society. The most dangerous criminal may be the man gifted with reason, but with no morals.*[6]

Over half a century later, take a look around you at our world today. His words still seem very fresh and very relevant.

---

6   M. L. King, Jr., The Purpose of Education. In C. Carson, R. Luker and P. A. Russell (eds), *The Papers of Martin Luther King, Jr. Vol. I: Called to Serve, January 1929–June 1951* (Berkeley, CA: University of California Press, 1992 [1947]), pp. 123–124 at p. 124.

STEP 2: IMPROVE TEACHER UNDERSTANDING OF EACH PHASE

'If you can learn a simple trick, Scout, you'll get along a lot better with all kinds of folks.' So says Atticus Finch to his daughter in Harper Lee's classic novel *To Kill a Mocking Bird*.[7]

The trick in question was that of empathy.

As mentioned earlier in the book, there is a growing chasm between primary and secondary schooling. At the heart of this disconnect there is often a misunderstanding of the different phases and of the roles, responsibilities and purpose of the schools and the teachers working within them. Despite being averse to being pigeonholed themselves, many teachers seem to hold strong stereo-typical views about the teachers who work at a different age range to themselves.

Too often I have heard primary teachers characterising secondary teachers as:

● Being more subject focused than pupil focused.

● Being overly ambitious for their own career.

● Possessing tunnel vision regarding examinations.

● Lacking knowledge of individual pupils.

● Favouring didactic forms of pedagogy.

● Being unprepared to try new ways of teaching.

---

7   H. Lee, *To Kill a Mockingbird* (London: Arrow, 1989 [1960]), p. 33.

Likewise, I have heard secondary teachers assume that primary teachers are:

● Focused on pupil welfare ahead of academic achievement.

● More likely to enforce less discipline in their lessons.

● More interested in the presentation of work than quality learning.

● Not interested in developing high-level skills in their pupils.

● Overly focused on the enjoyment of learning.

Before you shred this page and use it as hamster bedding, remember (a) don't shoot the messenger and (b) these are inaccurate stereotypes. However, as long as these sentiments exist, and others like them, the process of effective transition will always be more difficult than it needs to be. These crass assumptions grow out of a lack of knowledge of what actually happens in the other phase, with both groups of teachers often being so involved in their own work that they don't feel they have the time to investigate the realities of someone else's.

Too often, the only opportunities to meet colleagues from other schools are at evening meetings – frequently organised to address transition. In *Are You Dropping the Baton?* I suggested that the best way to damage relationships between the two phases of education is to hold a meeting between primary and secondary teachers to look at assessment levels between the ages in each subject.[8] This is not a view I have changed. I still see many well-intentioned meetings between schools which only serve to undermine relationships and reinforce existing stereotypes.

---

8   Harris, *Are You Dropping the Baton?*, pp. 65–67.

The best way to improve understanding of the work within each phase is not for teachers to sit and talk about it, but to *see* the other phases in action. Then, and only then, will all colleagues be in a position to discuss the differences they observe.

The following template may be useful to help teachers consider what to look out for when sharing each other's practice.[9] Teachers from across the phases should be paired up and encouraged to use this form on a joint learning walk. I recommend starting with the youngest learners and aiming to visit lessons in a chronological order across all the phases. The walks should be done in a spirit of research and mutual discovery, not judgement. This initial work is about finding out exactly what is happening currently. No more than a few minutes are needed in each class, and the overall purpose is to obtain a broad-brush overview of practice.

Sheet 1 can be used to gather evidence of practice at each phase visited:

Sheet 1 – Observations from learning walk	
Phase observed	
Question	Observation
How quickly does learning start?	
Do teachers recap the previous work?	

---

9   This template is based on a table that first appeared as resource G5(iii) in West-Burnham and Harris, *Leadership Dialogues*.

Sheet 1 – Observations from learning walk	
Phase observed	
Question	Observation
Are supporting materials displayed on the walls?	
What posters are on display in corridors?	
What posters are on display in classrooms?	
What specialist language is used in lessons?	
Is metacognition mentioned?	
How often do pupils have breaks?	
Can pupils move freely around the classroom?	
Do pupils put their hands up to answer?	
Do pupils write in notebooks?	
Is group work common?	
Do pupils work in silence for parts of the lesson?	
What do pupils do at breaktime and lunchtime?	
What are assemblies like?	

Sheet 1 – Observations from learning walk	
Phase observed	
Question	Observation
How are teachers referred to?	
How is attainment data used?	

Sheet 2 covers the same questions but is used to compare and contrast practice between the phases:

Sheet 2 – Pupil tracking summary: similarities and differences between schools		
Question	Similarities	Differences
How quickly does learning start?		
Do teachers recap the previous work?		
Are supporting materials displayed on the walls?		
What posters are on display in corridors?		
What posters are on display in classrooms?		
What specialist language is used in lessons?		
Is metacognition mentioned?		

Sheet 2 – Pupil tracking summary: similarities and differences between schools

Question	Similarities	Differences
How often do pupils have breaks?		
Can pupils move freely around the classroom?		
Do pupils put their hands up to answer?		
Do pupils write in notebooks?		
Is group work common?		
Do pupils work in silence for parts of the lesson?		
What do pupils do at breaktime and lunchtime?		
What are assemblies like?		
How are teachers referred to?		
How is attainment data used?		

Use sheet 2 to look for any trends in experience that are observed as the pupils increase in age and then record these findings on sheet 3.

Sheet 3 – Trends observed as the pupils' age increases	
Question	As the pupil gets older ...
How quickly does learning start?	
Do teachers recap the previous work?	
Are supporting materials displayed on the walls?	
What posters are on display in corridors?	
What posters are on display in classrooms?	
What specialist language is used in lessons?	
Is metacognition mentioned?	
How often do pupils have breaks?	
Can pupils move freely around the classroom?	
Do pupils put their hands up to answer?	
Do pupils write in notebooks?	
Is group work common?	
Do pupils work in silence for parts of the lesson?	

Sheet 3 – Trends observed as the pupils' age increases	
Question	As the pupil gets older ...
What do pupils do at breaktime and lunchtime?	
What are assemblies like?	
How are teachers referred to?	
How is attainment data used?	

Highlight in yellow any areas that show no clear trend or are broadly the same in each phase.

Highlight in green any areas that show a trend which you think is a positive one.

Highlight in red any areas that show a trend which you think is not desirable.

For the yellow trends (areas that are broadly similar across the phases), discuss how these can be built on. Where possible use a common language in each phase – for example, if pupils across all ages have a weekly focus for assemblies, such as personal, social, health and economic (PSHE) education, use the same name or even use the same focus in each phase. You should also aim to use the same language: calling a process 'marking' in one school and 'pupil feedback' in another misses an opportunity to emphasise connections. When pupils see the same language being used in both phases, they will recognise subliminally that the learning process is part of one continuous journey.

For the green trends (areas where the observed trends are positive ones), these should be celebrated and developed further. That said, if these trends do not fully align with the area's vision for education, as discussed in the previous section, then you have a problem. Either use these trends and build your ethos around them or change them to produce your stated mission. If your practice is already showing clear progression in the desired direction of travel, the following question becomes critical: how smooth is the trend you observed? In other words, is it a seamless progression from one phase to another or does it feel bumpier than necessary?

Not surprisingly, it is the red trends (where a trend is observed but is felt to be contrary to the desired direction of educational travel) that should be your main focus.

Let me give you an example: a group of schools have decided that their local education should be producing independent learners and have made this a focus of their vision statement. However, they have also identified that, as the pupils get older, they are given less responsibility in their learning and are being spoon-fed information. This situation – an example of what we might call undesirable age drift – must be addressed quickly. The schools need to clearly restate their desire for the pupils to gain more responsibility as they get older and to introduce an action plan with specific actions to do this.

It is important to remember that little things matter. Like genetic traits that show the links between different family members, schools in the same cluster should always look for ways to make visible the links between them and the fact that they are all part of the same family. The pupils will recognise these connections if they see conspicuous links to the work they have done in their previous phase. Examples here might include the use of similar motivational phrases, the same educational mnemonics (e.g. we are learning today (WALT), what I'm looking for (WILF), even better if (EBI), what a good one looks like (WAGOLL)) and labelling subjects in the same way (e.g. PE/sport/ games).

The act of studying learners' educational journeys will probably identify a number of areas where different language is used. This usually happens not because it is part of a deliberate plan, but because the schools have developed in isolation, as we discussed earlier.[10] For example, imagine this scenario: an infant school, a junior school and a secondary or senior school are all serving the same pupils and all providing education in a range of competences in addition to the traditional academic subject areas. Let's suppose they have used national guidance to structure this learning, thus ensuring that it is appropriate to the age of the pupils and forms part of a coherent learning journey from 5–16. However, the infant school refers to this education as life skills, the primary school as citizenship and personal education, and the secondary school as PSHE. Now, you may feel this is an insignificant difference, one that most pupils will quickly understand ('That's what we used to call ...') Of course, most of them will, but others, and I have met many, will not. For them, it all adds to the mass of educational verbiage they simply don't understand, and is yet another barrier between them and the success they want to achieve. What's more, such diverse terminology serves to reinforce and emphasise the differences between the different phases of their education – unnecessary bumps in what could be a smooth transition path.

When at least some of the teachers in all the schools have carried out the activities outlined above, it is vital that the information is shared and acted on. The stereotypes that prevail in primary and secondary schools will not be

---

10 You say potato; I say *Solanum tuberosum* of the Solanaceae family.

reformed without a clear and consistent strategy to do so. This strategy should include all of the following:

- A report outlining any identified differences and desired changes which is shared with all staff in each school.

- Sessions at staff meetings including input from each phase.

- Actions to address any issues raised should be considered at meetings in the schools and then revisited to check progress.

- Appropriate prompts placed in each staffroom.

- Increased understanding of each phase to be included in all school development plans.

Some schools have decided to take the process a step further. The National Centre for Excellence in the Teaching of Maths describe a secondary school in Croydon which employed a primary maths teacher to deliver secondary maths lessons.[11] They discovered that the benefits go wider than simply the teacher's own classes. When asked if they would recommend the process to others, they had no hesitation in saying yes. In the words of the school's head teacher:

> It involves a shift in mindset for the school and for the teacher involved. The school might find that its KS3 maths curriculum is not as challenging as it thought. The teacher must be able to adapt to the very different demands of teaching in a secondary school.

In other words, done well, this type of cross-fertilisation of ideas within and across schools can deliver great benefits

---

11 National Centre for Excellence in the Teaching of Maths, Why We Employed a Primary Teacher for Maths in Our Secondary School (11 April 2019). Available at: https://www.ncetm.org.uk/resources/53069.

in the classroom and the staffroom and is capable of having far-reaching effects. Which brings us back to Atticus Finch and seeing things from another person's point of view. As he explains wisely to Scout: 'You never really understand a person until you consider things from his point of view ... until you climb into his skin and walk around in it.'[12]

STEP 3: IMPROVE PUPIL UNDERSTANDING OF THE LONG-TERM GOALS OF THEIR EDUCATION

I have carried out numerous interviews with pupils across all phases of education in different parts of the world, and found a number of common themes running through the comments they make.

On education in general:

- Education is about me getting good exam results.
- Education is old-fashioned.
- I'm doing it because I have to.
- Learning is boring.
- School is about teachers telling us stuff.
- What use is [insert any number of subjects] ever going to be to me?
- My parents want me to go to university.

---

12 Lee, *To Kill a Mockingbird*, p. 33.

On primary schooling:

- The teachers knew us really well – I miss them.
- We often had lots of fun.
- We went on a lot of trips.
- It felt very cosy.
- It was very colourful.
- I didn't like the food.

On secondary schooling:

- It's all about exams.
- It's very strict.
- We see lots of teachers – some of them are really good.
- I really hate [insert subject] but love [an alternative subject].
- Behaviour is not good in some of my classes.
- The choice of food is good but it's too rushed/crowded.

On moving from primary to secondary school:

- It was very frightening but it wasn't as bad as I'd feared.
- It was confusing to meet so many new faces at once.
- I was upset that I wasn't with [friend X] in any classes but always seemed to be with [nemesis Y].
- I kept getting lost.
- It was very confusing at times.
- The first thing the school did was to make us do exams.

- In some subjects we did some really easy things; in others we didn't understand it.

These snippets are not presented as a definitive record of every child's experience of the move from primary to secondary school, but they do represent some frequently voiced opinions that I think many teachers will recognise. Of course, some pupils are innately resilient, and the whole process of changing school is an exciting adventure that they thoroughly enjoy. However, when I encounter pupils who are very positive about the transition experience and ask them about possible improvements to the process, they tend to highlight ideas similar to those I have listed.

Food quality aside, the reality is that when pupils are asked to compare and contrast their experiences in primary and secondary school, they find it much easier to list the differences than highlight the similarities.

While this may well be a natural response to any new experience – visit a new country and its differences to your own will strike us first – we must not lose sight of the fact that for many young people their experiences of primary and secondary school are ones of contrast. The two schools differ in numerous significant and minor ways (and lots of little things add up to one big thing), and their day-to-day learning experiences bear little resemblance to each other. My view is that we should be looking for ways to eliminate these differences as much as possible in order to better facilitate the process of transition.

As in step 1, confusion about the purpose and point of education is at play again here too, and it is as prevalent in young people as it is in their teachers. For some, the moment of greatest misunderstanding about the purpose of schooling happens around transition. If pupils are allowed to think that serious learning only begins at secondary school, then they are being encouraged to believe that whatever they did at primary school didn't really count and they need to start again – and do it properly this time. Sadly, I am aware of teachers in both primary and secondary schools who have played their part in perpetuating this myth and allowing jaded stereotypes of the phases to appear real.

If pupils can be encouraged to believe that their schools are working together with a common goal, then there is a greater chance that they will observe the recurring themes in their education. If the schools have produced a common educational mission, as outlined in step 1, this should be central to the work in each school. This vision should be explained in clear, simple language and should be visible in all aspects of the day-to-day school life. At the very least, the same statements should be displayed at the entrance of each school, underlining to all concerned that 'this is what we are all about'.

Of course, laminated values change very little. As my Independent Thinking colleague Mark Finnis has observed, 'If your values are on a lanyard around your neck, they're probably not your values.'[13] It is important that pupils witness at first hand the same ethos in each school and experience the same attitudes and beliefs. If a child believes that their new teacher has no knowledge of their past learning successes (and challenges), they will believe either that it can't have been very important after all and/or the new teacher (and indeed the whole school) doesn't really care about them.

Imagine the following scenario:

_____

Adya has been at primary school for seven years. In that time she has come to understand that learning

_____

13 See https://www.independentthinking.co.uk/associates/mark-finnis.

can be fun, but also that it needs to be taken seriously. Learning is something active, done by and not to her, and she feels that she has a say in what and how she learns. She has been told many times that the life skills she learns are as important as the examination results she receives. Her experiences at school have led her to believe that this is true, and she has repeatedly been given a lot of 'adult' responsibilities by her teachers.

Adya is sad about leaving her old school behind, but she is also excited about all the opportunities that lie ahead for her at secondary school.

Her first week of secondary school consists of her sitting formal tests (cognitive ability tests (CATs), BKSB tests, etc.) to assess her 'actual' ability. This leaves her assuming that her secondary school doesn't trust her primary school. She is a perceptive girl and starts to wonder, perhaps my primary teachers haven't done a good enough job? Perhaps I'm not as good at school as I thought I was? Perhaps I'm going to be found out?

She is quickly put into top sets and is told that she is expected to get high grades in her GCSEs in five years' time, and that her journey to them starts today. She starts to think that going to school is all about exam results.

She finds her new classes very formal compared with those in her primary school. The pupils have to sit in single lines and in alphabetical order. Many of her initial lessons are spent writing the rules for learning in that subject. She reasons that perhaps 'real' learning is not meant to be fun.

In most of her new subjects she isn't allowed to work in a group, and the teacher spends a lot of time speaking to the class as a whole. There seems to be a great deal of writing and not much opportunity to talk and discuss the learning. A quick learner, Adya begins to realise that the best way to learn must be for the teachers to talk and for her to listen.

This scenario is being replicated in schools across the world; rarely deliberately and usually through the type of osmosis described here.[14]

It doesn't have to be this way.

In some secondary schools Adya's experience would have been very different:

In her first week Adya would not have sat any tests. All her teachers would have spent time with her primary teachers and would have seen examples of her work. In some cases, she would be continuing work that she began in primary school. Her new teacher may even refer to conversations held with her previous teacher.

The secondary school would have a transition curriculum in place (overseen by teachers from the feeder primary schools), and for much of the first week Adya would remain in a single classroom, undertaking projects and group work across a

---

14 At this stage we must ask ourselves the question, what is education for? Is it simply about the greatest number of young people with the highest number of good grades at GCSE? Or is it about more than that? In other words, as we like to ask at Independent Thinking, what are they learning while you are teaching them?

range of subjects, similar to the approach she experienced in her previous school. Her primary teacher might even pop into her class one morning to check on how everyone is doing.

In this example, Adya genuinely experiences the connections between the different parts of her schooling rather than focusing on – and potentially being overwhelmed by – the differences. It's like going to a new country and seeing Cadbury's chocolate fingers in the supermarket!

Please note that if planning a whole new curriculum is a step too far for your school, any moves you make to show a common approach will not be wasted. I will highlight a number of ideas and suggestions in step 4, but please be assured that each and every time a pupil experiences a positive link with their previous school, you will have succeeded in making transition that little bit easier.

STEP 4: ENCOURAGE OPPORTUNITIES FOR PUPILS OF DIFFERENT AGES AND PHASES TO LEARN TOGETHER

Birthdays are an artificial construction – becoming one year older has no magic significance. One year just happens to be how long it takes the Earth to circle the sun, something that happens to take just over 365 rotations on its own axis (or days as we call them).

Yet in the school system we bestow on a birthday some mystical meaning that is linked directly §to what and how a child should be learning and who they should be learning it with. If we were to continue with that logic, when we open up a new multi-academy trust school on Mercury, a term would last about 30 Earth days and pupils would move up a year every three months. The Saturn branch, on the other hand, would have children moving up every 29 Earth years.

I make these points not to flaunt my science background, but to emphasise that the concepts of day and year have no intrinsic meaning. They are simply a product of the size and gravity of our home planet and our distance from the sun. In this light, how can we suggest that we all progress neatly in year-long units and need an abrupt and all-encompassing transformation to the way we learn, and the building we do the learning in, when we move from one extra-magical unit to the next?

Schools of all phases expect a certain level of work from particular groups of children who have been brought together by their ages – or, at least, the parameters within which their birthdays fall – even though there may be a greater age difference within a school year group than between individuals in different year groups. For example, a child born just inside the school year cut-off date will only be a few weeks older than one born just the other side of that date, but the two will be treated as if the elder one is a whole year more mature for the rest of their educational journey.

This takes us back to the brain, where we started our journey, and exposes that the basic age-based foundation of schooling in most countries is grounded in misconceptions and misunderstandings. The human brain does not develop in a linear manner, and the rate and nature of brain maturation and development varies greatly between individuals.

This was a clear advantage offered by the one-room school, mentioned in Chapter 1, where children were able to plot their own learning path based on their prior knowledge, interests and abilities, and were not simply given work dependent on their biological age. There are clear advantages, therefore, for schools which have the wisdom to begin breaking the stranglehold of age-related learning. What's more, these positive outcomes are not just limited to the process of transition. Children of all ages experience improved learning – and learning outcomes – once the work is matched to their actual needs rather than to their perceived needs.

I know of a number of small rural primary schools which have been obliged to create mixed-age groups due to budgetary and logistical restraints. Although some of these schools initially experienced parental resistance to the prospect of their child being in a group with older/younger children, most of these concerns disappeared once the parents found that the type of teaching which is most successful across a mixed-age group – engaging, group-focused work with scaffolded support at a variety of levels – actually produced better outcomes for their child.

When a school is keen to loosen its reliance on age-determined learning (e.g. an 11-year-old learns one thing, while a 12-year-old learns another), a suitable first step is to focus the initial work within that school itself, completely divorcing it from transition. This ensures that the staff understand that this is about improving the learning of the children in their care. It is not about other schools; it is about *their* pupils.

Aim to start small to begin with and encourage teachers of adjacent age groups to deliver a day-long project across the two year groups. Choose a topic that is new to both groups and ensure that the work will benefit from a mix of ages. Encourage teachers to provide learning that relies heavily on group work, problem-solving and investigation. They should observe the learning and identify the key differences between the different age groups. Discuss the findings at a subsequent staff meeting. It is extremely likely that the teachers discover that the pupils will quickly focus on the learning involved, and that any differences in attitude, approach or ability within year groups will be just as large as those between them. Once the school has dipped its toe in the water of mixed-group teaching, hopefully there will be a positive attitude towards developing it further.

The next stage for a primary or secondary school wishing to become less reliant on teaching towards age-related expectations is to identify opportunities for pupils of different ages to collaborate in their learning on a weekly basis. If possible, timetable classes of different ages in the same space. These types of changes may initially cause mass eyebrow-raising in the staffroom and a whisper that the head is trying to save money, but in my experience the benefits quickly emerge.

When I instigated joint Year 9 and 10 options for some GCSE subjects I received a few visits from teachers who were worried this wouldn't work. Some feared that their results would take a dive. 'Year 9 are just too immature,' said one. 'It will take twice as long to cover the material, and I don't get any more time in which to do it.' In fact, the reality turned out to be quite a surprise for this particular sceptic, and he actually found that the mix of pupils worked very well, with both groups seeming to motivate each other. The work was completed more quickly and their understanding of the topic seemed greater. On examination results day he could not hide his pride as his mixed-age group obtained the best results he had ever seen. In his words, 'I was sure this wouldn't work but I am delighted it did. I want all my classes to be like this.'

So, all well and good within an individual school. But what happens when we come to implement mixed-aged teaching across schools in different phases as part of an agreed transition process?

We have already seen how one of the objectives of a transition programme is to remove the idea that learning should suddenly transform at a set age. Therefore, the more opportunities a pupil has to work with others who are not of the same age, the more chance there is that they will appreciate that all their schooling is connected.

An obvious place to start may seem to be to set up a project linking pupils from either side of the primary–secondary divide, and of course this is possible. However, there are some barriers to successfully linking up these two groups of learners. The pupils might be in different schools now, but they may well have grown up together or even be siblings. What can happen – and it is an entirely natural outcome – is that the secondary pupils 'play the expert' to the primary pupils, which can totally change the dynamic of the exercise.[15] By contrast, I have seen a programme that linked Year 8s with Year 5 and 6 pupils which was incredibly fruitful. The children are close enough in age to learn together without being so close that power games raise their head.

Another caveat is that the focus of any such multi-age endeavour must not be 'this is how we do it at big school' but on real learning *together*. For some – children and their teachers – it is a bombshell to discover that sometimes it is the youngest child in the group who produces

---

15 I frequently see the same phenomenon when primary and secondary heads share the same conference. Just saying …

the most insightful learning. I clearly remember an example of this when the all-through school I led held a whole-school science week, as part of which cross-age teams were given joint projects. Observing the work was enlightening. The youngest in the groups did not sit back and let the oldest pupils complete all the work, as you might fear. Instead, an enthusiasm for the task was the dominating feature among all the learners. Older and younger pupils explored ideas jointly. Some of the oldest pupils (often reluctant to be seen to be actively engaged in their own classes) weren't worried about showing positivity for the work. The pupils were laughing and learning. Furthermore, the links these projects forged between pupils of different ages were not limited to the science week, but remained within both the school and the wider community.

As a scientist, much as I would like to suggest that it was the focus on science that made the magic happen, a week-long multi-age event could focus on any number of areas. Other possibilities I have come across include:

- Local history projects.

- Developing local area walks.

- Renovating a garden play area.

- Responding to local environmental issues.

- Providing evening entertainment for the community.

- Producing a 'wonder space' for the area (more on this in Appendix 2.3).

All of these topics will benefit from being considered by pupils of different ages, and you may well observe that the most innovative ideas emerge from the youngest pupils who have not yet learned the 'rules' of school.

I have no doubt that if a group of schools were to enthusi-astically launch a series of joint projects, it would greatly help the transition process *and* increase knowledge of the abilities and potential for learning across the ages. However, this should be seen as just the beginning, some-thing that only scratches the surface of what is possible. The really serious school will find ways to build mixed-age group learning into their day-to-day curriculum.

STEP 5: DEVELOP A CURRICULUM PLAN FROM INFANT TO ADULT FOR YOUR GEOGRAPHICAL AREA

Having followed the first four steps, you will now have: a common vision for education in your area, teachers and young people who understand this vision and their role in it, and pupils who realise that learning is not something you only have to do with people of your own age. The next step is to provide a skeleton around which all this flesh can form.

First, list all the subjects, topics, skills and attitudes that will be needed to produce your educational vision. Here are some possibilities to start you off:

- Literacy.

- Numeracy.

- Science.

- History.

- Geography.

- Languages.

- RE.

- Art.

- Music.

- Drama.

- Sport.

- ICT.

- Design and technology.

- Citizenship.

- Health education.

- Sex and relationships education.

- Open-mindedness.

- Resilience.

- Social awareness.

- International mindedness.

- Problem-solving skills.

- Ability to reflect.

- Risk-taking.

- Caring for others.

Once you have identified the essential components of your curriculum, you need to get teachers from each phase who are responsible for each topic to sketch out possible progression routes in that area. It is important to stress that the ideal result is not a ladder of skills and abilities; learning is rarely as simple as this. What you are seeking to produce is something more akin to a spiral. The advantage of a spiral curriculum, as opposed to a linear one, is that it builds in the revisiting of areas and skills. The learner is given the opportunity to strengthen their understanding and then expand upon it.

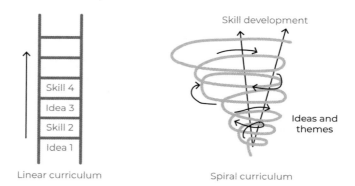

Linear curriculum

Spiral curriculum

Spiral planning is not particularly easy in two dimensions, however, so the table on page 65 provides support for this process.

Note: at the moment there is no mention of ages or phases – just learning.

It is important to focus not on who will be delivering this teaching but whether it is a skill worthy of development.

I can't deny that this type of detailed transition planning represents a considerable amount of work, but I would reassert my view that it is effort well worth making. The research backs up my claim too. For example, Dr Ria Hanewald of Australia's Deakin University investigated the effectiveness of transition programmes over a six-year period between 2005 and 2011. She found that pupils who participate in transition programmes go on to have higher assessment scores than those who have none: 'Students participating in a primary to secondary school transition

Topic					
Development of key ideas in this topic	Key progression of skill 1	Key progression of skill 2	Key progression of skill 3	Key progression of skill 4	Possible resources

program had higher outcomes for academic effort than their peers who did not participate.'

What's more, the teachers involved in the programmes benefitted too: 'Teachers involved in the transition program had sustained levels of positive efficacy for meeting the instructional, behavioural and social needs of all students compared with teachers in the control group, who did not participate in the transition program.'

Effective transition also seemed to have an impact on non-academic areas, such as improving the behaviour of students who had previously shown aggressive tendencies: 'Students with higher levels of aggression who were participating in the transition program tended to socialise more with academically productive peers than students with higher levels of aggression in the control group.'

The key reasons for this effect, she suggests, seem to be the building of stronger relationships between pupils and between pupils and teachers and a greater sense of belonging to the new institution. She also sums up precisely why I'm urging schools to invest time in the transition process: 'teachers are critical in this passage from primary to secondary schools'.[16]

---

16 R. Hanewald, Transition Between Primary and Secondary School: Why It Is Important and How It Can Be Supported, *Australian Journal of Teacher Education* 38(1) (2013): 62–74 at 68.

STEP 6: BUILD LEARNING EXPERIENCES BETWEEN THE PHASES INTO THE CALENDAR

We nearly all do it. We wait until the week before (or the day before) someone's birthday to begin looking for their present. We leave choosing our outfit for that special occasion until the hour before we go out. We make that dental appointment just after the point when the tooth starts aching.

On the whole we are reactive creatures, leaving things to the last moment and dealing with what is in front of us rather than what will inevitably be there. We address the urgent rather than the important. For much of our life this trait does not lead to any major problems (apart from the odd domestic shouting match). We cope. However, in the case of transition coping is not good enough. This is not something we can afford to let slip by.

Almost every primary and secondary head teacher I know will say, without hesitation, that they want to prioritise transition work. They recognise its importance. The problem is that because transition is not seen as time critical it falls into the important but not urgent box. It is something that can be put off until next week, next month, next term. The intention may be to hold a number of events, but other priorities with tighter deadlines (exams, tests, reports, inspections, etc.) conspire to keep transition at the back of the queue.

This is the reason why any school which is serious about getting transition right needs to take control of the calendar and schedule events throughout the year, and not just before the pupils are about to move institutions.

What follows is a series of suggestions to add to your school calendar that I hope will get you started. It is not a definitive list, nor is it written in stone. They are simply some ideas to help you get your thoughts in order before you sit down with the draft calendar for the next academic year.

- **Termly meetings between primary and secondary teachers to share plans for each area of the curriculum.** Ensure these meetings are both productive and amiable (perhaps increase your budget for biscuits!). Staff building relationships can only be positive for the process of transition. Even purely social events are likely to be an asset. Remember, the surest way to make these meetings fail is to use them to focus on moderating grades between the phases.

- **Joint curriculum day events between primary and secondary schools.** Ideally these should not be limited to the classes either side of transition, as we saw in step 5. The wider the age range of pupils working together, the more they will accept that they are on a coordinated learning journey, and the more seriously they will take their learning. I have included a number of possible ideas for joint curriculum days in Appendix 1.1. It is important that these events do not only occur at the secondary school; rather, the pupils should work in a variety of locations, which will emphasise the fact that learning happens everywhere and diminish the opportunity for any perceived hierarchy of importance between primary and secondary phases.

- **Joint project weeks between primary and secondary schools.** Again, these should involve as wide an age range of pupils as possible and be situated in both primary and secondary school locations, and possibly across the community too – museums, galleries, parks and libraries (if you're lucky enough to have one). The work should arise out of the detailed curriculum planning described in step 5. See Appendix 1.2 for some joint project week ideas.

- **Regular use of each other's facilities.** Try not to make this all one-way. Avoid the secondary school appearing like some benevolent relative and emphasise that this is about having an equal partnership. If a primary school has the space (often at a premium, I realise), turn it into an area that can be used by all ages. You will find further ideas in Appendix 1.3.

- **All-age tutor groups.** If you are feeling particularly brave, schedule some weekly (or fortnightly for the more timid) multi-age tutor groups with pupils from both primary and secondary phases in which you focus your activities on building relationships between the different ages. These groups can be very effective when it comes to delivering elements of the PSHE/ citizenship curriculum. Topics particularly suitable for dealing with in a mixed-age group are broad ones such as respect, leadership, identity, community and the environment. A mixed tutor group would also be the perfect setting for increasing pupils' understanding of neuroscience in terms of developing learning – for example, you could get them to explore areas around growth mindset, neural plasticity and the amazing potential of every brain. More details can be found in Appendix 1.4.

- **Pupil–teacher days.** These provide schools with an opportunity to focus on encouraging peer-to-peer teaching. This will not just be within groups of the same age but also between year groups and also between primary- and secondary-age children. It is important to highlight that older pupils 'educating' the younger ones is not the only way to arrange peer-to-peer instruction. In fact, I have seen some very successful examples of younger pupils in the role of instructor for older ones. More details can be found in Appendix 1.5.

- **Schedule weekly 'teach to learn' opportunities, where older pupils facilitate the learning of younger pupils in particular subject areas.** These should not be 'special events' but rather a regular part of the learning process for both younger and older pupils. At its most effective, older pupils develop their higher-level understanding of a topic by revisiting more fundamental elements with the younger ones, while the younger pupils benefit from a fresh perspective on the topic. More details can be found in Appendix 1.6.

- **Teachers from both primary and secondary phases identify curriculum areas where there are topics suitable for both schools.** Particularly suitable areas might be English, maths, science, art and PE, but almost any area is a possibility. This method can produce win-win opportunities on a social and educational basis for a large number of pupils.

It is worth noting here that, while little research has been carried out into this quite rare type of activity, a study into peer-to-peer interactions by Ian Morrison and colleagues did identify the positive nature of such activities. The researchers found that while there was 'no clear pattern of improvement in the language skills of either group of tutees ... both felt more positively about reading'. They also identified that through the peer-to-peer process, 'relations between younger and older pupils were developing in positive ways'.[17] Building confidence in reading and improving relationships between young people counts as a double win in my book, and I'm sure in yours too.

- **Joint school trips.** When a potential visit is being planned, aim to include pupils from both phases of education. This will serve to build positive relationships between the ages (and the teachers involved). Furthermore, it will not only enforce the idea that great learning can happen away from the classroom but it will also remind older pupils that it is OK to enjoy their learning.

- **An area-wide school council.** Take pupils from a variety of ages across both primary and secondary schools and form a monthly schools council. At the first meeting, give them training on the role of pupil councillors and the need to both inform and gather opinions. Make it clear that the group is not just a talking shop, but that it is expected to make a discernible impact on the community. Ask the pupils to try to identify communal and community issues that could feasibly be tackled by the group. (There may need to be some initial work to help the children recognise what is realistic and what is not, but this is all part of the fun. And, remember, just because you don't think it can be done, doesn't mean that a group of cross-age children can't do it!) The pupils should canvass opinions from their classmates and then, at a further meeting, choose one item on which to focus the council's efforts. The project should be given biscuits and a budget, and the pupils should be

---

17 I. Morrison, T. Everton, J. Rudduck, J. Cannie and L. Strommen, Pupils Helping Other Pupils with Their Learning: Cross-Age Tutoring in a Primary and Secondary School, *Mentoring & Tutoring* 8(3) (2000): 190-197 at 190.

encouraged to publicise the work and its impact as widely as possible. This method can produce benefits in many areas, including transition, citizenship, community cohesion and relationship-building across the age ranges.

STEP 7: MAKE SURE YOUR INDUCTION PROGRAMME IS A SUBSET OF YOUR TRANSITION PROGRAMME

As mentioned in the introduction, many schools make the mistake of thinking they are doing transition when all they are really doing is induction. That is like confusing the fire drill with the fire. If you have read this far you will know that transition is much more involved than this. That doesn't mean to say that induction activities are a waste of time – absolutely not. It is just that these important activities, which usually take place in the gap between SATs (or equivalent) and the summer break, need to form part of a much longer and more detailed transition process.

When it comes to getting induction days right, the first step is to identify what it is you wish to achieve from them. Possibilities might include:

1   Increasing knowledge of the buildings, their nomenclature, layout, routes and restrictions.

2   Clarifying the new school 'way of being' – that is, the school rules but couched in more positive language.

3   Increasing familiarity with the secondary staff, their names, roles and codes (if appropriate).

4   Increasing understanding of the rhythms and procedures of the school day, including breaktime and lunchtime procedures.

5   Getting pupils used to a more formalised system of lessons, responding to bells and moving between rooms and teacher rather than staying in one classroom.

6   Administrative issues such as checking contact details, medical records, payment and registration systems.

7   Introducing pupils to their timetable for the first term.

8   Checking and clarifying expectations for uniform and equipment (sporting and specialist).

9   Introducing and building relationships between pupils from different primary schools who will be classmates at secondary school. This may include new registration groups and subject classes.

10 Reducing apprehension and fear for the start of the new term and building a sense of expectation for the new school (as long as this doesn't involve the 'Now your learning *really* starts' mantra).

11 Helping pupils to realise that their learning is a continuation of their primary school work, rather than pushing the idea that the work in every subject will be very hard/very exciting/very different/all of the above.

12 Answering questions and dispelling myths. It is upsetting to discover how many pupils on the verge of moving to secondary school will have taken to heart stories of rituals involving having their head flushed down a toilet ('having a swirly' as it is apparently known). I have met dozens of pupils who report having heard this story but none who have had it happen to them (thankfully). However, FEAR (false

expectations appearing real) can be destructive, whether based in reality or not.

With this list of 12 essentials as a starting point it is easy to see how vital induction days are (and also how important it is to refrain from throwing subject learning into the mix). However, it is of enormous benefit to spread out this type of information over the months (and years) as part of a comprehensive transition process.

You will notice one deliberate omission from the list above, and it is one about which I must make a very heartfelt plea. Please do not use induction days to carry out ability testing (CATs, BKSB, etc.). Not only does it waste valuable time (there is plenty to be getting on with in the 12-point list already) but you also have to think about the potential negative messages it sends out to new pupils:

- You don't trust the primary staff.

- You are going to label them based on the result of a test and put them into sets or groups accordingly.

- Their intelligence is fixed.

- Education is all about exams.

- We must be silent to learn.

Once you have agreed that tests are not on the induction to-do list, I suggest you approach the 12-point list (you may have more) in a holistic manner rather than as a series of lessons to deliver. Possibilities could include:

- A passport to success activity: a number of activities need to be completed and 'stamps' achieved before pupils are ready to enter the next stage.

- A forensic science day.

- A wonder and curiosity day.

● An arts-based day.

● A themed day.[18]

Remember that many (if not most) pupils will encounter some type of stress as they move from an environment they are familiar with to somewhere new. They need to be helped to understand that this is a normal process and that the feelings they have are normal too.

Geoffrey Borman from the University of Wisconsin-Madison led a team who investigated ways to address this. Even though the research was targeted on transition to middle school in the United States, there is nothing to suggest that it would not apply equally to primary–secondary transition. One group of transitioning students were given no intervention and another group were given structured literature tasks relating to their feelings about and personal experiences of transition. The objective of the study was to help students realise that concerns about 'fitting in' are not only entirely normal and to be expected but also are usually short-lived. There were significant results for the group who experienced the transition support: disciplinary incidents reduced by 34%, attendance increased by 12% and the number of failing grades reduced by 18%.

According to Borman, the reasons for these striking results were clear: 'The kids internalized this message, they worried about tests less, they trusted their teachers more and sought help from adults … They also felt like they belonged in the school more, and because they felt more

---

18 See Appendix 2 for a more detailed description of these activities.

comfortable, they didn't act out as often and they showed up more.'[19]

This type of focused activity – which could be a structured literature task or something else entirely – can be introduced into any of the tasks outlined in this chapter. It would seem that encouraging pupils to talk about their fears helps to dispel them quicker. Who would have thought?

19 University of Wisconsin-Madison, Power of Refocusing Student Stress in Middle School Transition: Sixth Graders Taught to See Transition Turmoil as 'Normal, Temporary' Perform Better in Class, *Science Daily* (29 July 2019). Available at: https://www.sciencedaily.com/releases/2019/07/190729164630. htm. See also: G. D. Borman, C. S. Rozek, J. Pyne and P. Hanselman, Reappraising Academic and Social Adversity Improves Middle School Students' Academic Achievement, Behavior, and Well-Being, *Proceedings of the National Academy of Sciences of the United States of America* 116(33) (2019): 16286-16291.

CHAPTER 3

SUCCESS FACTORS

Now I have described my seven steps to getting transition right, it is worth bringing into the equation some other factors that also have a part to play in the success or otherwise of the transition process.

THE ROLE OF PARENTS

According to research carried out as part of the School Transition and Adjustment Research Study (STARS) project by University College London and Cardiff University, schools and pupils are not the only participants in the transition experience: 'Parents were an important source of support over the transition period and results suggested it was helpful for parents and pupils to discuss their concerns.'[1] Parents and guardians are a very important group who should not be forgotten. Opinions and attitudes experienced within the home environment are readily absorbed by developing minds, and fears and concerns held by parents are often mimicked by their children.

Among other important findings, the STARS study identified that 'parents have a good understanding of their children's needs in that parents and children tend to agree about what is most concerning for pupils – specifically

---

1   F. Rice, N. Frederickson, K. Shelton, C. McManus, L. Riglin and T. Ng-Knight, *Identifying Factors That Predict Successful and Difficult Transitions to Secondary School* (2008), p. 5. Available at: https://www.nuffieldfoundation.org/sites/default/files/files/STARS_report.pdf.

homework and friendships'. Interestingly, they also high-lighted the power of positive parental engagement in transition: 'Parental expressions of warmth and affection have a long-term influence on how self-controlled children are which in turn affects how well they do at secondary school both in academic and behavioural spheres.'[2]

In other words, engaging parents in the transition process at an early stage is likely to produce tangible benefits. Sharing the long-term aims of the collaboration between schools will help to cement the concept that education is a coordinated journey, and that all the teachers are committed to doing everything they can to help every child along the way. The STARS team suggest that schools could produce leaflets and booklets to help parents in this endeavour. I have also seen examples of schools forming parent support groups which can help to identify potential problems before they manifest themselves and serve to build confidence and trust in the school system.

SEN PUPILS AND TRANSITION

I (and many others I meet) believe that an unintended consequence of our increasingly data-driven, tick-box education system is an increase in the numbers of young people who find this style of learning neither suitable nor straightforward. Sadly, there are children around the world who are being judged (and, worse, judging themselves) to be academically unsuccessful, when in fact it is the way their learning is being delivered that is wanting.

---

2 Rice et al., *Identifying Factors That Predict Successful and Difficult Transitions*, p. 21.

While at face value it might appear that the term SEN (special educational needs) is self-explanatory, to whom does it actually apply? I would argue that at some point in our education journey all of us will have 'special needs' of one sort or another, when we find some aspect of learning more demanding than those around us. It is at this stage that we require additional support. In this way, the ideal SEN department in the ideal school will have a file on every person in the building. As Monty Python fans will remind us, we are all individuals.

Of course, some pupils have very complex mental, physical and developmental needs, and I would not want to down-play the importance of focusing on these during the transition process. If a pupil is used to one-to-one support, or to having their work printed on yellow paper, or to having low levels of noise in the classroom, arrangements must be made to ensure a similar experience in the next phase of their learning. Thankfully, in most countries there are systems in place to support this, including planned induction arrangements and regular meetings between staff with SEN responsibilities.

Often, the induction and transition procedures for those who might be described as having high-level needs are far more advanced than for those who have lower level needs. For example, the Autism Education Trust recommend including details about the following in a 'transition pack':

- *New environment – maps, locker, bells*

- *New expectations – break/lunch times, transition between classes*

- *New vocabulary – 'tutor group', 'head of year', subject-specific vocabulary*

- *Key people – mentor, form tutor, SENCO, who/how to ask for help*

- *Quiet area – library, allocated area for stress management*

- *The timetable – how to use it, formatted for the individual's understanding*

- *Systems for organization – diary, checklists for materials and books*

- *Homework – expectations and explanations*

- *Transition workbook – addresses differences between primary and secondary school, and new experiences with a step-by-step approach ...*

- *Personal profile – written by pupil (with LSA [learning support assistant]/parent/teacher support), includes all the information new staff should know about the pupil.*[3]

It is also worth bearing in mind that, even with a national SEN code of practice, it is not uncommon to find pupils who are identified as SEN in one phase of education but have no classification at all in the next phase. We have already identified the potential dangers of poorly arranged transition for any pupil and this is magnified many fold for those with any form of serious learning need. For example, if a child has been identified by their primary school as having issues with concentration, for which they receive short breaks every hour, entering a secondary school which is unable to provide similar provision will result in the process of transition being far from satisfactory. It is therefore essential that a system is designed not only to ensure smooth transition for children with complex and serious needs, but also one that can share the subtleties of learning need experienced by all pupils about to embark on transition. The strengths and weaknesses of every child

---

3   A. Stobart, *Transition Toolkit: Helping You Support a Child Through Change* (London: Autism Education Trust, 2016), p. 10. Available at: http://www. learningsupportcentre.com/wp-content/uploads/2016/01/Autism-Education-Trust-Transition-Toolkit.pdf.

should be assessed. And by this I don't mean that they simply are set another test. When the focus of transition is based around test scores, it is almost inevitable that the nuanced vision of the whole child is diminished.

Transition for SEN pupils can produce problems for which solutions must be agreed across both schools involved in the process. I know of one situation where a primary school developed a wonderful profile of each pupil, including any preferences for learning conditions. Each record gave a vivid three-dimensional profile of the child focusing on both their strengths and weaknesses. The work involved in these evaluations was immense, but it was clearly born out of affection for each child. You can imagine the frustration and dismay when the primary head teacher visited the secondary school half way through the following year and spotted a pile of these files, covered in dust and still tied up with the original string. The damage done to inter-school relations, and consequently to children's learning, can easily be imagined.

GENDER EFFECTS IN TRANSITION

I certainly would not want to reproduce some ancient stereotype of 'what girls want' or 'what boys want' from transition. Every child is different and could not and should not be boxed in by gender.

That said, to claim that every child in the world receives an education completely without gender bias would be insane. We live in a world in which assumptions and prejudices bleed out of every action and organisation. Girls and boys do not always receive the same educational experience, so it is inevitable that they will have different experiences of transition.

In a survey I carried out covering 300 pupils across five secondary schools, a few interesting trends emerged. For example, when asked what message they would send themselves, if they could magically go back a few months before transition, this is what they said.

Typical answers from the boys were:

- Prepare for loads of homework.

- Don't worry about being bullied.

- Don't be scared.

- Have fun.

- Don't worry about the older pupils.

Typical answers from the girls were:

- Don't worry about the teachers.

- Friends are important.

- Don't worry about being small.

- Don't worry about being embarrassed.

- Be more confident.

When asked what message they would send to their secondary teachers to improve the experience of transition, typical answers from the boys were:

- Don't forget we have only recently started.

- Don't give us too much homework.

- Please try to be nice.

- Help people more.

- Don't shout too much.

Typical answers from the girls were:

- Let pupils learn in their own way.

- Know us better.

- Be more helpful.

- Teachers should know our names.

- Ask our primary teachers about us.

When asked what they would improve about the education system, typical answers from the boys were:

- Not so much homework.

- Make learning more fun.

- Don't do tests.

- Make your own timetables.

- Keep the same teacher.

- Have shorter days.

Typical answers from the girls were:

- Make it more like primary.

- Ban swearing.

- No tests.

- More involvement in own timetable.

- Have more transition events.

- Spend more time getting to know your teachers.

Unsurprisingly, there is no earth-shattering difference here in the way boys and girls view transition. Everyone expresses concerns about the amount of homework and an overemphasis on tests. Dislike for the formal arrangements of the curriculum is also evident across both sexes. However, there are some interesting insights. For example, we can see that, for the boys, many of the issues are around practicalities – the organisation of the day and of their learning; by contrast, the girls responses are often focused on relationships, in particular relationships with their teachers.

The key message in this book is about developing a fluent transition process (and subsidiary induction programme) that works for all, and which helps to remove the uncertainties that arise from moving to a new school and building relationships with new teachers.

For another perspective on this contentious area, it is worth looking at Ros McLellan and Maurice Galton's detailed survey into pupil well-being during the transition process.[4] They apply a systematic statistical approach to considering what they refer to as eudaimonic well-being ('functioning well') and hedonic well-being ('feeling well').

The authors conclude that schools should look to a model from occupational psychology, so the transition process would consist of four distinct phases:

1   Preparation: this would be what we have discussed under the banner of induction.

2   Encounters: learning how to be a successful student – for example, through learning-to-learn courses.

3   Adjustment: 'frequent and immediate feedback' on progress and settling in (not punishment and correction).

---

4   R. McLellan and M. Galton, *The Impact of Primary–Secondary Transition on Students' Wellbeing* (Cambridge: University of Cambridge and Nuffield Foundation, 2015). Available at: https://www.educ.cam.ac.uk/people/staff/mclellan/Final-Report-June-2015.pdf.

4   Stabilisation: the student setting 'social, personal or academic' goals related to him or her making the most of their time at the new school (not punishment and correction).[5]

While it is suggested that this model could benefit all pupils involved in the transition process, the report also highlights that the ubiquitous drop in well-being experienced by all young people between the end of Year 6 and the end of Year 7 was more pronounced in girls than in boys:

> *The difference between girls and boys in terms of the self-reported eudaimonic wellbeing is concerning as it suggests girls feel less able to succeed and flourish in life, suggesting that despite the fact that girls overall are out performing boys in school, ... schools still need to support girls specifically.*[6]

Whether a school decides to plan specific support by gender is an interesting challenge, even without adding further complexities now that many schools are beginning to better understand and embrace gender and other LGBTQ+ issues. However, to completely ignore the matter would seem unwise.

---

5   McLellan and Galton, *The Impact of Primary-Secondary Transition on Students' Wellbeing*, p. 51. See also N. Nicholson, The Transition Cycle: A Conceptual Framework for the Analysis of Change and Human Resource Management, *Research in Personnel and Human Resources Management* 5 (1987): 167-222.

6   McLellan and Galton, *The Impact of Primary-Secondary Transition on Students' Wellbeing*, p. 20.

BACK TO FIRST PRINCIPLES

Many of us cut our educational teeth on Maslow's hierarchy of needs, and while it has its detractors these days, it is still incredibly useful as a model for much of schooling, especially transition.[7]

A typical representation would be:

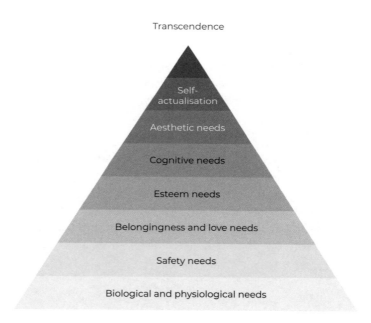

Transcendence

Self-actualisation

Aesthetic needs

Cognitive needs

Esteem needs

Belongingness and love needs

Safety needs

Biological and physiological needs

MASLOW'S HIERACHY OF NEEDS PYRAMID

In *The Little Book of Big Stuff About the Brain*, Dr Andrew Curran explains how an increased understanding of neuroscience helps to back up the implications of Maslow's

---

7   A. H. Maslow, *Motivation and Personality* (New York: Harper & Row, 1954).

work.[8] He explains that both dopamine and glutamate need to be present in the brain for learning to happen, and how stress creates too much dopamine, as well as a number of other chemicals, which hamper positive learning. The best way to produce a neurological environment conducive to learning is to help young people to feel rewarded by learning or feel the anticipation of reward. He suggests four simple steps: (1) understand the learners in front of you, (2) build their self-esteem, which will in turn help to (3) build their self-confidence, and then (4) engagement and learning will naturally follow.

Focusing on cognitive needs before biological needs is as ridiculous as choosing the curtains before building the house. I recommend that any school or group of schools looking to create the very best transition process in their area would do well to start with Maslow's famous hierarchy. It is important to prioritise meeting the biological and physiological needs of the pupils before all else. This can be as simple as ensuring that the pupils' food and drink needs are addressed from the outset, and not just as an add-on to the process. I once heard of a pupil who didn't know where the toilets were in their new school, and so didn't eat or drink for the hours before or during the first visit. They fainted and were taken home. This experience tainted their relationship with the secondary school for many years. Ensuring that pupils have a positive experience of the toilets and the food in their new school is a sensible priority.

Schools which believe that a one-day induction is all that is needed to effectively transition their new pupils are trying to achieve the top on the pyramid without first securing the base. When schools simply focus on levels of

---

8   A. Curran, *The Little Book of Big Stuff About the Brain: The True Story of Your Amazing Brain* (Independent Thinking Series) (Carmarthen: Crown House Publishing, 2008), chapter 4.

achievement, new timetables, curriculum organisation, staff names, room layout, daily systems and so on, they are working in the cognitive realm without having first enabled the pupils to feel safe, secure and loved. When looked at through the perspective of Maslow's hierarchy, the benefit of a long-term approach to transition becomes clear. When pupils develop an extended knowledge of the secondary school they are moving to over a period of time, including an understanding that what will happen is part of a continuous educational journey and a belief that the new school has the same values as their current school, they are developing the lower levels of the pyramid. These are the foundations on which we can build a genuinely successful transition process.

FINAL THOUGHTS

The increased distance between primary and secondary phases should be of real concern to us all.

I have recently witnessed examples of real ignorance from some secondary teachers towards primary education, and from some primary teachers towards the issues and demands of secondary education. This mutual lack of understanding damages our pupils and in turn limits the potential of the whole education system.

My own understanding of the potential of quality transition came when I helped to form an all-through school (infant, junior and secondary). Once we had embarked on this wonderful project, it became obvious that learning should be focused on the child and not about the individual phases. It remains for me the most child-centred form of education. However, despite my experience in, and passion for, all-through schooling, there is a good reason why I have not written a large section about it for this book. It tends to scare people.

Whenever I mention it at conferences, I feel a collective clenching of buttocks as people look nervously around them. For many it is a step too far. This is unfortunate. However, I would like everyone to realise that all-through schooling is not an essential part of a great transition; it is just a nice outcome of an exceptional one.

When the relationship between primary and secondary schools has become so strong that they want to work together more closely, that is when an all-through school should come into the conversation. Only when leaders, governors, teachers, parents and pupils all see the sense of a single school should it happen.

All-through schools that are a by-product of local reorgan-isation, an attempt to address failing institutions or a rationalisation of resources are typically doomed to an unhappy life. All-through schooling should not be built on money-saving contingencies, but on a joint passion for providing a seamless educational journey.

When all-through schools happen for the right reasons (which is very rare), they can produce the purest form of education – a place where pupil learning is front and cen-tre for the whole of their time in school. In addition, teachers will move seamlessly between the different ages, sitting in whatever staffroom they feel like. They will not congregate in cliques at staff meetings and will be keen to work with pupils of every age. Teachers may be given responsibility for learning across a broad age range and encouraged to find ways to support children, regardless of their birthday. A very good all-through school will be iden-tified by the laughter in the corridors and the success in the community.

If you are one of those overwhelmed by the thought of joining together schools, please do not allow this to put you off improving transition. Choosing just one of the ideas in this book (or those in the following appendices) is much better than doing nothing. Anything which helps to build a stronger relationship between the phases of edu-cation is worth doing. Having the will to improve the situation is perhaps the biggest ingredient.

A well-known quotation (attributed to Martin Luther King, Jr. and others) comes to mind: 'Take the first step in faith. You don't have to see the whole staircase, just take the first step.' In other words, while planning is good, wanting to do something and then actually doing something about it, is more important.

Please take that first step!

JOINT ACTIVITIES

1.1. JOINT CURRICULUM DAYS

EGG RACE

OVERVIEW

This is a stand-alone day with an interesting problem-solving task at its heart – an egg race. No formal pre-learning is required for the event, and the exact nature of the activity should be kept from the participants until the day. Mixed-age groups are given identical materials and time to solve the task in front of them. This will contain elements that will allow most pupils to fully engage. Points (and prizes) will be awarded not just for solving the problem but for evidence of group work and artistic interpretation. An account of the day's learning, with accompanying photographs, should be displayed in all the schools, ensuring that the benefits spread beyond the event itself. The nature of joint curriculum days means that it is unlikely to be possible to hold an event big enough to involve whole year groups from each school in one day. While it would be ideal for as large a number of pupils to be involved as possible, if it is not, ensure that the photographs and reports from the day are shared with the whole student body. It is also possible to hold heats in each school, with the most successful pupils making it to the day, or for those schools really committed to transition there could be a series of egg challenges, allowing all pupils to be involved over a two-year period.

DETAILS

Location: If possible, avoid making the location for the event the secondary school. Unconsciously, this can make secondary participants feel that they are 'in charge', and it may make primary children less keen to become fully involved. A primary school hall can often be suitable, but given their multifunctional use a local community hall may be the most successful venue. If the secondary school is the preferred location, work hard to make the space special for the day.

Theme: There are many excellent possibilities for an egg race. In the pages that follow I detail three of my favourites, each with the resources required.

TRADITIONAL EGG RACE

Using a wooden egg (considerably less messy and prone to misuse than the real thing!), a limited selection of every-day materials and a set time to complete the task, the groups must construct a device to propel an egg down a slight five-metre incline in the quickest possible time. Points will be awarded for the best time, artistic flair and evidence that all group members have contributed.

Resources for the whole event:

- Five-metre track (or suitable alternative).
- Something to raise the track to give it a very slight incline.
- Stop clock.
- Score chart.

Resources for each group:

- 1 wooden egg.

- 10 sheets of A4 card.
- 2 large sheets of thicker card.
- 3 toilet rolls.
- 10 short lengths of wooden dowel rods (10cm).
- 2 longer lengths of wooden dowel rods (20cm).
- 10 elastic bands.
- Sellotape, scissors, staples, glue, coloured pens, string.

Instructions: Before the event, select balanced groups containing a full range of pupils across the ages involved (e.g. a group of eight might be made from two each from Years 4, 6, 7 and 9).

Begin the day with some simple warm-up activities, which will encourage the pupils to get to know each other and set a positive mood for the task. The groups then move to their allocated table, on which the materials have already been laid out. Explain the task to the group, show them the racetrack and describe the judging criteria. Emphasise that no one is allowed to push the egg carrier down the track – it must move on its own. The groups then spend 15 minutes away from the worktable, during which time they must discuss how they are going to approach the task. An additional rule that may help to ensure the success of the event would be to insist that the oldest pupils cannot be the group leaders. Each group should be given an A3 scrapbook to record their ideas and workings.

After the planning time the groups are given one hour to construct their egg carrier. Each group then demonstrates their invention to the whole group and explains how each member has been involved. The groups are allowed two goes at the five-metre course, taking the best time from the two attempts. The fastest group is awarded 10 points, the second fastest 9, and so on. The best design is awarded in a similar way. The groups are also awarded a further mark out of 10 for how well they worked as a team. The groups should be encouraged to produce a record of their experience to be displayed in the schools, showing what they have learned about the task, each other and working in a group.

TOWER BUILDING

A suitable object (e.g. a wooden egg) must be held for a minimum of 10 seconds at a height greater than 30cm from the desk. The higher the suspension, the better, with points being awarded for height, design and teamwork.

Resources for the whole event:

- Two-metre stadiometer/ruler with a horizontal marker (as used to record an individual's height).

- Clock.

- Score chart.

Resources for each group:

- 1 wooden egg (or equivalent object – each group must have the same).

- 5 sheets of poster paper.

- 10 sheets of A4 card.

- 10 sheets of A4 paper.

- 25 straws.

- Egg box.

- Ball of string.

- Sellotape, scissors, stapler.

Instructions: Before the event, select balanced groups containing a full range of pupils across the ages involved (e.g. a group of eight might be made from two each from Years 4, 6, 7 and 9).

Begin the day with some simple warm-up activities, encouraging the pupils to get to know each other and set a positive mood for the task. The groups then move to their allocated table, on which the materials have already been laid out. Explain to the group that they must design and build a structure which can hold an egg at least 30cm off the desk, maintaining its stability for at least 10 seconds without any contact. For those who complete the task there is a bonus point for every centimetre above 30cm the group achieves.

The groups then spend 30 minutes away from the worktable, during which time they must discuss how they are going to approach the task. Additional rules that may help to ensure the success of the event would be to insist that the oldest pupils cannot be the group leader and that there must be evidence that every group member has participated. Each group should be given an A3 scrapbook to record their ideas and workings.

After the planning time the groups are given one hour to complete the construction. No height measuring will be done until the hour is up. The order of the groups is then chosen by lottery and each group makes a brief presentation explaining their design and showing the roles of each group member. The presentation should be made by at least one member from each phase. Following this the group will be given one minute to demonstrate their structure. The height will be measured by the judge and a ten-second counter will be used to ensure it is stable enough to score.

Each group is given a mark out of 10 for design and for teamwork, plus 10 points if their 30cm structure can hold an egg for at least 10 seconds. Bonus points are awarded for every centimetre above 30cm that is securely constructed (e.g. a 44cm structure would achieve 10 + 14 = 24 points).

If time allows, there is an excellent opportunity to follow up this challenge with some cross-phase life skills work. Using the different solutions the children have come up with, interrogate the decisions made and how many risks the group took. For example, some groups may have decided that it was better to build a smaller and more stable structure, close to 30cm, and to focus on getting the maximum design and teamwork scores, while others may have decided that building a tall structure was the key – did this risk pay off? You could then ask each group to design a poster to represent their learning from the day – about building structures, working in a team and taking risks. The findings can then be shared with wider groups back at the schools.

ROCKET RACING

Each group must design and build a rocket which will travel across a hall on a guide wire in the quickest time/ greatest distance. The 'power' for the rocket will be provided by deflating balloons. Points will be awarded for the quickest times, rocket design and evidence of whole-group participation.

Resources for the whole event:

- A line running from one side of the hall to the other plus a tube that is free to move along the line (e.g. a strong plastic straw). The line could be made from string but to ensure smooth running it is preferable to use wire or nylon (e.g. plastic strimmer line). The line should be easily accessible at both ends and drop slightly towards the finishing point. It is important that when propelled the tube can move at least a few metres along the line. A strong piece of card should be securely attached to the tube – this is how the rockets will be secured to the line.

- Tape measure to determine distance travelled (or ruled marks along the line).

- Clock.

- Score chart.

Resources for each group:

- Kitchen/toilet roll tube.

- 10 sheets of A4 card.

- 10 sheets of A4 paper.

- Cotton wool/scrap paper (or equivalent packing material).

- 5 assorted balloons.

- 10 straws.

- Bulldog clips (or equivalent to hold the air in the inflated balloon).

- Sellotape, duct tape, stapler, felt-tip pens.

Instructions: Before the event, select balanced groups containing a full range of pupils across the ages involved (e.g. a group of eight might be made from two each from Years 4 ,6, 7 and 9).

Begin the day with some simple warm-up activities, encouraging the pupils to get to know each other and set a positive mood for the task. The groups then move to their allocated table, on which the materials have already been laid out. Explain to the groups that they must design a rocket which can travel across the room using only balloon power. To ensure it travels in a straight line the balloon will be tethered to a tube on the wire.

The groups then spend 30 minutes away from the worktable, during which time they must discuss how they are going to approach the task. An additional rule that may help to ensure the success of the event would be to insist that the oldest pupils cannot be the group leaders. Each group should be given an A3 scrapbook to record their ideas and workings.

The groups are then given one hour to complete their build. Not only must they think about the most aerodynamic shape, the best way to attach the balloon to the rocket, the best way to attach the rocket to the wire, the release mechanism and the ideal weight of the rocket, but they must also try to make it look attractive. No testing of the rocket is permitted during this hour.

After the build, all groups are put in a lottery to choose the order of rocket testing. When it is their group's turn at least two members of the group (one from each phase) will explain their design, why they have chosen it and how they approached the task as a group. While this is happening two other members of the group will be attaching the rocket to the string and 'arming' the balloon.

Following a countdown, the rocket will be launched. If it completes the full distance the time will be recorded. If it does not travel the full length of the line then the distance will be noted. Scores are awarded out of 10 for performance (10 for the fastest/furthest travelled, 9 for the second, etc.), for the design and for the way the group worked together.

Set aside some time after the activity for the groups to discuss how they would approach it differently if they were going to start the task again, what they have learned about the task, what they have learned about each other and the benefits they have found from working together. Their findings should be captured and shared in all the schools.

THEMED ENVIRONMENT DAY

OVERVIEW

It has probably always been the case that the young possess a greater passion for environmental issues than older generations; those who stand to be affected the most will be the ones who feel the need to act more acutely. As evidence grows that the world stands on the brink of an environmental catastrophe, it is young people who are pressing for action, so this topic should provide an excellent focus across the whole age range.

Many educationalists feel that schools should be covering the climate crisis in the formal curriculum, although the coverage is currently very limited.[1] The reference (if brief) to environmental issues in the national curriculum does set the stage for projects where ecological and climate related projects can become a focus. In a stand-alone day the objectives must be clear but they must also not be too broad. I would recommend that the environmental focus chosen is rooted in the community of the schools – so although it may be impossible to solve the issue in a day, some significant impact can be made. Irrespective of their age, young people can become very passionate about their own community. This will enable pupils from different

---

1   See, for example, https://www.independentthinking.co.uk/associates/professor-paul-clarke.

schools (and phases) to work together more quickly than if a traditional subject was chosen as the focus for the day.

DETAILS

A lead teacher should be chosen in each school, with the main credentials being an understanding of the numerous environmental issues facing the planet and more specifically their own community. The teachers should meet at least a couple of months in advance of the proposed day. As mentioned previously, try to avoid holding the meeting in the secondary school and also try to avoid it being chaired by a secondary school teacher. These may seem like pedantic points, but it is out of situations like these that stereotypes and assumptions arise.

The meeting should try to identify a theme which will be of interest to pupils from across the age range. It is important for the steering group to remember that this is about having a positive, enjoyable day, and not about changing the world in 24 hours.

Possible themes could include:

- Designing a garden for a communal plot of land.
- Collecting rubbish from the area and then creating artworks from the waste.
- Producing posters/leaflets for local shops encouraging shoppers to use 'bags for life'.
- Designing and producing green 'bags for life'.
- Monitoring traffic/pollution and creating a campaign to encourage less car use.
- Designing a reward scheme to encourage recycling.

- Devising practical solutions to the traffic chaos which occurs outside many schools at the start and end of each day (e.g. walking school bus).

- Analysing the waste and recycling from each school and trying to find ways to improve this.

- Carrying out a simulation for a larger issue – for example, if a benevolent billionaire donated £50 million, how could it best be used to reduce pollution in the area?

Whatever the theme chosen, build an enthusiasm for the topic in each school in advance of the day. Encourage pupils (and teachers) to start talking about the issue and gather views and ideas.

For the day itself, plan for groups of six to eight pupils, split between the schools involved and across as wide an age range as possible. Start the day with some 'getting to know you' icebreaker activities. A short keynote or video related to the topic might also help to stimulate their interest.

It is important to give enough structure to the task to avoid pupils feeling lost, but enough space for them to produce something they 'own' and not to feel as if they are reproducing what is in the teacher's head. It will be beneficial to have some adult support to help any groups who get stuck, but this help should not be given too quickly. The talented speaker Jonathan Lear (see www.independentthinking.co.uk) often describes the light-bulb moment when he and his teachers realised that when pupils are given a task with 'desirable difficulty' they will often find the solution on their own – *if* they are allowed to make mistakes and not be guided too quickly by teachers.

Award points for the outcomes from each group, although a large component of these marks should be for the way the group works together. For example, you could offer bonus points if it is not the oldest pupil who becomes the leader. Perhaps members of the local community affected by the issue could also be part of the judging team for the day.

It is essential that there are many outcomes for this event: booklets, letters, posters, newspaper articles, photographic displays in each school and in the community and possibly even a roadshow which spreads the work further. This instantly produces a connection between the schools involved and ensures that the positive messages of the day are not forgotten in the bustle of daily life. The local press is often keen to get involved in events which have different schools working together, and the potential of a positive environmental impact is an additional bonus. Any publicity that connects primary and secondary schools, and demonstrates that they are working together for the local good, can only be of huge benefit for transition.

ART/MUSIC/DANCE EVENT

OVERVIEW

This is an excellent opportunity to show how well pupils of different ages can work together. When I was leading an all-through school, we organised a Samba Day where pupils aged 8–18 worked together with a travelling musician. Memories of the day are of laughter, enjoyment, learning and a lot of noise! The trainer contacted me after the event and said that it had been the most enjoyable workday of his career. He described how the presence of the younger pupils gave the older pupils 'permission' to be fully involved, and remarked on how maturely the primary pupils behaved in the presence of their secondary peers.

DETAILS

Form a planning group with representatives from each school. As mentioned previously, try to avoid holding the meeting in the secondary school and/or having it chaired by one of its teachers. Some groups of schools opt for a particular medium for the arts day, such as painting or singing. However, if your goal is to involve as wide a group of pupils as possible, a subject theme can be more effective so the pupils can respond in whatever medium they choose (e.g. one group may dance while another may produce a large piece of art). The key focus of the day should be on 'doing' rather than being 'done to'. The day may include some training or guidance in particular skills, but the benefit from the day should derive from pupils of different ages being able to express themselves creatively.

The list of possible topics could include:

- Our community.
- The environment.
- Working together.
- Equality.
- Empathy.
- The brain.

Alternatively, the steering group might prefer a curriculum topic of joint interest – for example, basing an art event around an element of the maths curriculum could produce many benefits.

Once the group has decided on the intended topic focus for the day and the medium(s) that will be permitted, the teachers can start work on their long-term plans. This type of event works best when pupils engage with it as part of their normal curriculum, which enables very large numbers to participate. The planning group should also agree criteria for who can take part in the special transition day. This should not just be about artistic excellence, but also about imagination, enjoyment and, of course, inclusion.

It is essential that the artwork is put on display as an exhibition (or exhibitions). Ideally, work from all the pupils involved (of every age) will be exhibited in each school. If there is a single exhibition, this should preferably be in a community venue where you can maximise the number of people who get to see it. Artwork and photography may be the simplest mediums to display, but it is not difficult to set up a video loop of music or dance performances which can be shown on the entrance screen of each school.

I would avoid making the event competitive and instead focus on making it a celebration of talent. If prizes are awarded, try to make them about the values demonstrated during the event and not about finding the 'best' artist.

The event at the heart of an art day should contain two elements: some cross-age learning (possibly via external input) and an opportunity to share the range of work completed over the preceding weeks. Engaging an external facilitator (e.g. the samba trainer mentioned on page 102) to hold a half-day session for a mixed age-group of pupils will be a catalyst for conversation and enjoyment. It will also be new for all the pupils involved, which will enable them to have the same fresh relationship with the teacher. It is also important to set aside some time to celebrate the artistic work being completed in the day-to-day life of each school to ensure that all the pupils understand that their learning is not just a disconnected event, but part of a joined-up process.

The planning group should meet up after the event to determine how it could be further improved in the future, and also to identify new pupil interest groups that could be set up between the schools – for example, street dance, photography, samba, pastels.

COMMUNITY EVENT

OVERVIEW

A group of primary and secondary schools advertise and arrange a special event in the local community. The event may have no overt connection to transition or learning, but the process can be hugely beneficial for the pupils involved and can cement the idea within the local community that learning is a connected journey. Most of the examples in the previous section could be extended into a community event. The positive here is that instead of focusing on the relationship between the schools and on the process of transition, the community is the focal point, and improved transition just one of the many benefits.

DETAILS

Most schools will have a member of staff who is responsible for liaising with the local community, someone who will have clear ideas about the current needs, wants and passions of people in the area. These individuals may already meet up as a school cluster, as in many areas groups such as these are used to access community funding grants. This group should be tasked with identifying events that the community does not currently hold but might enjoy. Some schools have community coffee groups which can bring about a symbiotic relationship: not just focusing on what the school needs from the surrounding area but also what the school can provide for the community. The most effective events are likely to be ones that evolve from this type of collaboration, which will ensure that the community feels listened to rather than being given things they don't want or need.

Possibilities for invents include:

- Street party (for a special event).

- Tea dance.

- Fashion show.

- Exhibition of local history.

- Keep-fit classes.

- Language cafe.

- Line dancing classes.

- Community sports day.

- Taster sessions for unusual sports/games.

Once an event is agreed on, detailed planning should occur involving staff and pupils from all the schools. While the planning group will inevitably manage much of the fine detail, the event itself should directly involve as many pupils as possible from across the complete age range. Pupils can be organisers, hosts, co-learners, presenters, waiters and so on; the importance is not so much on what they do but that they are involved, and are seen to be involved, and meet as many new people as possible.

In this era of data-focused priorities it is easy to avoid being involved in community events for fear that it is not directly impacting learning. However, these types of event improve community relations, help pupils of different ages meet and work together, and demonstrate to the local community that their schools collaborate, helping to create a very positive climate for learning.

1.2. JOINT PROJECT WEEKS

THEMED SCIENCE/HISTORY/ MATHS[2] WEEK

OVERVIEW

This is a week in which a particular subject becomes the centre of learning in each school. The week will work best if the focus is not too general – for instance, an aspect of a subject rather than the whole thing (e.g. fractions rather than maths). Teachers will plan work in individual classrooms, within each school and across the whole partnership. Pupils and teachers will move between schools and there will be some elements of cross-phase learning. The work will be celebrated across the community and the joint approach will be publicised widely.

DETAILS

The first step is to have a meeting between senior curriculum leaders in each school (possibly the head teachers – this initiative needs to have high status). The purpose of the meeting is to identify an area of the curriculum that would benefit from a week of high profile activities. Let's assume that the group identifies science as an area that all the schools would like to support. The next stage is to call a meeting of staff with responsibility for science in each school, whose task will be to agree on an aspect of science which has common themes across the whole age range. This could be a subdivision of the subject (e.g. anatomy or astrology) or a topic which could be visited at many different levels (e.g. air, light, weather).

---

2   Insert any appropriate subject.

Once the focus has been decided on, the staff in each school should produce a plan for how this could form the centre of a week's work within their own area. At a subsequent meeting of the group, ideas should be shared and plans for joint events built around the chosen themes. A plan of the learning objectives to be covered in each school should be produced and disseminated.

During the week there should be a variety of events across the whole community. These might include:

- Guest experts.
- Pupil experts – pupils sharing their knowledge with children of a different age. (Remember, this doesn't have to be limited to older pupils teaching younger ones.)
- Parental/community events.
- Displays in each school or community buildings.
- Topical newspaper written by a multi-age panel of pupil reporters.
- A problem-solving day (similar to the suggestions in Appendix 1.1).

A very effective finale to the week is to stage a joint event, where a small group of pupils from each school work together to set up 'stalls' to share their learning from the week. Pupils from all the schools can visit the displays, and parents and members of the local community can be invited too.

One of the schools I've worked in developed this idea very successfully when we concluded a science week across the area cluster with a two-day Air Fair. At this event pupils from Years 6 and 8 set up table-top experiments and displays connected to the theme of air/gas in the local community hall. We also invited along experts in the field, such as lecturers from a local university to demonstrate liquid air, workers from British Gas who used old gas pipes to build goal posts, a pneumatics company and even a parent mending bicycle tyres! Children and adults working together with the common goal of making science fun. Each school was given a timeslot to bring along pupils not directly involved in the event, and there were early evening sessions each day which were open to anyone in the local community. A mixed group of primary and secondary pupils were given the task of recording the day, with photographs, interviews and recordings being used to produce a newspaper called 'Air News'.

My memories of the Air Fair are very positive: the pride of the pupils demonstrating their experiments to others, children from different schools working together effectively and, most of all, the palpable enjoyment in the learning. Themed days certainly involve considerable effort, and I understand why although many school leaders might feel this is a laudable event, they feel they cannot justify spending their valuable time making it happen. I would simply ask if there is anything more important than increasing pupils' interest and knowledge in a subject, reducing their fear of meeting pupils of different ages, building bridges between the staff of different schools and fostering positive community relations.

1.3. REGULAR USE OF EACH OTHER'S FACILITIES

OVERVIEW

Many secondary schools encourage linked primary schools to use their specialist facilities – music, science, art, drama, technology and sports. While these experiences can be positive for transition by building primary pupils' knowledge of the secondary setting, I am also aware of some instances where the process has damaged relationships. Too often the facilities are not available at the most appropriate time and often only for a limited period. In addition, the logistics of fitting these visits into the timetable can cause conflict between teachers rather than fostering partnerships.

DETAILS

The sharing of facilities works most successfully when both schools plan visits into their weekly timetable, thus allowing for the use of specialist rooms to be integrated into their learning plans. This requires goodwill and planning at a senior level in both schools. However, even when the logistics are handled perfectly there is a danger that the process can produce a hierarchical relationship – the secondary school is *kindly allowing* the primary to use its facilities. Incorporating the needs of other schools into curriculum planning ensures that it is an essential part of the process and not just an add-on.

One way to produce a more balanced relationship is for the primary school to make some of its facilities available to the secondary on a regular basis too. Initially the primary school may feel its own amenities are not appropriate for older children, but there are some spaces that may be of great worth to secondary schools. These might include:

- A community room. Primary schools often have strong links with the community and so have a dedicated meeting room. This could be invaluable to secondary staff and pupils wanting to meet with local people.

- Kindergarten/early years provision. Structured access to early years facilities can be extremely useful to secondary pupils, not simply in directly related topics such as child care but also in core areas where stages of learning are being discussed. Older pupils helping infants to learn can be a very effective way to consolidate their own studies.

- Greenhouse/garden facilities. Horticultural activities are an excellent vehicle for younger and older pupils to work together and can be connected to many parts of the curriculum. Secondary pupils can link it to science, maths, business studies or even enterprise work. Voluntary qualifications such as ASDAN fit perfectly with these types of opportunity.[3]

- A vocational room. Some older primary schools may have smaller rooms which they don't use on a regular basis (I apologise for those of you in schools where you don't have room to breathe!). If you do have an underused room, why not ask if the secondary school would like to use it for some vocational work – perhaps they are looking to set up a beauty salon, engineering room or literacy hub. Having a facility onsite which is used regularly by older pupils can help to reduce fears about transition.

---

3   See https://www.asdan.org.uk/.

WONDER ROOM/CORRIDOR/CUPBOARD

Before explaining how wonder and curiosity could be the backbone of the transition work in your schools, I will briefly expand on its development in education.

I know of a number of schools which have embraced the concept of wonder in learning, and each one of them is a place to behold – you could even say, wonder-full! Using curiosity and wonder as prompts for learning has its roots in the cabinets of curiosity of the 16th century. These were collections of unusual items, often from nature, that would go on public display – objects that would widen an individual's perspective and encourage them to embrace new knowledge.

I was introduced to the modern version of the wonder room by Independent Thinking's Dr Matthew McFall.[4] Matthew has inspired many schools (both primary and secondary) to allocate an area of their building to hosting a collection of interesting items. Some schools have a dedicated wonder room, but those lacking space have used cupboards and corners of halls very effectively. In St Catherine's school in Sheffield, for example, they have even developed a corridor of curiosity.

At its best, the collection (whatever format it takes) should be available for pupils to visit, both as part of their formal learning and outside lesson time. Typical objects that might be found in a wonder area include:

- Animal skeletons.

- Unusual plants and their seeds.

- Rocks, minerals and fossils.

---

4   See M. McFall, *The Little Book of Awe and Wonder: A Cabinet of Curiosities* (Carmarthen: Independent Thinking Press, 2013).

- Pieces of old science equipment (e.g. Galileo thermometer, periscope).

- Clockwork/mechanical toys.

- Old household equipment (e.g. rotary dial telephone, typewriter).

- Puzzles (new and old).

- Optical illusions (2D and 3D).

- Insects.

- Interesting mirrors.

In fact, you can include almost anything. At my school we had a 'Shelf of Boredom', and made the rule that objects could only stay on it if everyone agreed it was boring. Nothing ever lasted long!

The secret of success for wonder areas is as much about the presentation and setting as the items themselves. I have seen collections set up using little or no budget; the pupils' level of interest is rarely linked to the amount spent on the display. The most popular item I have seen was a handmade box with the letters of the alphabet painted onto a grid into which woodlice has been placed. The pupils would visit to see which letters the woodlice were resting on and try to 'decode' the words they could be spelling out!

Wonder is an excellent hook into learning and seems to be indiscriminate of age or ability. Matthew McFall has discovered that pupils with learning challenges (such as autism) find wonder areas an inspiration, but also that older pupils (and adults) are captivated by its contents. Pupils will often focus on an object that fascinates them and quickly become an 'expert' on it. I recall watching an 11-year-old taking huge pride in demonstrating the solution for a wooden puzzle to a university professor who was stumped by the object. Some schools have taken this idea further and have appointed pupil 'curators of curiosity', who develop, curate and staff the display.

For these reasons, wonder and curiosity make a perfect focus for transition work.

DETAILS

When a school spotlights wonder and curiosity, it is automatically creating a learning resource for all ages. Pupils of different ages (and even adults) can interact with the same objects in ways that suit their particular needs at that particular moment. A 9-year-old and a 13-year-old can both be fascinated by the same object. A wonder area in a primary school could be the focus for cross-phase learning, and in a secondary school it could be a resource to support aspects of the science curriculum.

There are three basic ways to integrate the concept of wonder into a transition programme:

1 Jointly build a wonder room, either in one school or a community area. Involve pupils from all the schools when deciding what will go into the room and also on its design and curation. Each school should aim to use the room as frequently and in as many different ways as possible. The goal is for the room to feel like a shared space.

2 Create a community wonder trail. Ask the pupils to create a series of wonder questions (the questions in Appendix 3 should help to start them off) or observations which highlight interesting places or events in the local area. These questions will appear at specific locations indicated on a map. Wonder trail participants will follow the map, attempting to answer

the questions at each checkpoint. Involve pupils from different ages and schools in preparing the questions and materials to support this activity.

3   Hold an event like those described in Appendix 1.2 but make the focus wonder and curiosity. The aim of the day could be to identify ten curious or wonderful things in the local area, or for each school to work together to produce a cabinet of curiosities.

The advantage of using wonder and curiosity in transition is that, while it is not on the national curriculum, it underpins all learning. Rarely will an event lead to the repetition of any planned work in the schools, but it will reliably support positivity for learning across the full range of subjects.

1.4. MULTI-AGE TUTOR GROUPS

OVERVIEW

The practical and logistical complications surrounding forming a regular meeting of pupils across the age range stops many schools from making this happen. Indeed, some schools that have dabbled with this idea have decided that the benefits are not worth the effort. However, other schools see it as one of the most powerful things they do. I believe that success depends on the way it is implemented.

The core reason for setting up a multi-age tutor group is to strengthen relationships and to build an understanding that learning is a process we can all do together. It is not a set of boxes to be ticked but a journey we are all on. Therefore, the focus of the work carried out in a mixed-age tutor group setting should be based around conversation and collaboration, not on more didactic forms of learning. Successful mixed-age groups will look at themes which apply to every age – issues that are not simply parts of the curriculum but skills and concepts that are useful for life. Topics might include:

- Empathy.

- Trust.

- Values.

- Problem-solving.

- Resilience.

- Mindfulness.

- Community.

It is important that the work is not simply a set of teacher questions designed to lead the pupils towards a learning goal, where the only aim is finding the correct answer. This type of activity will simply establish an age hierarchy where the older pupils are likely to find the answer in the quickest time. Activities which require everyone to put forward an opinion, to listen and to collaborate will produce the best results. For example, if the mixed-age group were given the task of choosing how to spend a £25,000 grant on a local play area, the viewpoints and ideas of everyone in the group would be required. The teacher's role is to facilitate and then to help the group to identify the skills they have used in the process. Some schools that have embraced this type of learning have found tangible benefits for the process of transition. Developing relationships between individuals in different age groups helps to reduce anxiety in younger pupils, improve some unwanted behaviours in older pupils and can reduce incidents of bullying.

It is very important that parents are fully informed about the cross-age project; in the absence of facts it is easy for parents to develop unnecessary concerns. They need to be told why the groups are being formed and what the pupils will (and will not) be looking at. Parents may also need to be reassured that younger pupils are not learning 'bad habits' from older students.

1.5. PUPIL–TEACHER DAYS

OVERVIEW

Type 'co-construction of learning' into your favoured web browser and you will be swamped with results. Whether it is an article by the National College for Teaching and Leadership or a blog post by Tom Sherrington, there are many examples of schools trying to shift the leading of learning away from the teacher towards the pupil. Like most things in life, co-construction is probably not the answer to all our problems but, equally, it will have elements that are worthy of further investigation.

Too often, pupils are passengers on a journey designed by their school and teachers. However, many schools are finding that giving pupils responsibility for setting their own direction can have very positive results. When young people are given the opportunity to play a more active role in what they learn, the order in which they learn it and how they learn it, there is often an immediate improvement.

One of the strategies successfully adopted by some schools is to use pupils to 'teach' their peers, which many claim is more effective than a teacher-focused model.[5] In

---

5   See, for example, S. Briggs, How Peer Teaching Improves Student Learning and 10 Ways to Encourage It, *informED* (7 June 2013). Available at: https://www.opencolleges.edu.au/informed/features/peer-teaching.

the context of this book, we can see the benefits for transition of utilising aspects of peer-to-peer teaching. Asking older pupils to plan the learning for and with a younger age group is an obvious first step. Giving a group of 14-year-olds the task of helping some 8-year-olds to develop their use of verbs will consolidate grammar for the older pupils while also providing a positive learning environment for the younger ones. However, there are real merits to turning this process on its head and asking younger pupils to lead the learning of older ones. Obviously, you need to choose the topic carefully, but there are many areas where learning does not have to be one fact placed after another. In other words, an individual section/lesson can be taught in isolation from the previous learning. Topics that are built heavily on the teacher's input in earlier lessons are therefore less suitable for this type of activity. I have observed younger pupils very successfully helping older pupils to think about topics such as values and imagination, and I once saw a primary group very effectively teach a group of older secondary pupils about De Bono's Six Thinking Hats.

This type of activity could be of benefit in any school, and clearly it does not have to be confined to special events. The advantage of identifying a common collaborative day across all schools is that it ensures that this does actually happen. When involving work between the ages, if the experiences are well planned and the learning opportunities tightly defined the learning can be impressive. The benefits that emerge from the event will hopefully have a knock-on effect in the day-to-day practice of all the schools.

1.6. WEEKLY 'TEACH TO LEARN' OPPORTUNITIES BETWEEN SCHOOLS

OVERVIEW

These are regular timetabled sessions where older pupils become facilitators for the learning in a particular section of the curriculum for primary children. They plan their input with the primary teacher but also in partnership with the secondary teacher responsible for their own learning in that area. This works best when the older pupils deepen their learning in a subject, cementing some of the foundations, and the primary pupils benefit from a fresh perspective.

DETAILS

Facilitate meetings between the staff responsible for the learning in the subject on which you wish to centre the work. I have seen English, maths, science and PE all work extremely well. Ask the primary staff to identify a section of the curriculum they think would be suitable for the secondary pupils to work on with their pupils. This will ideally be a specific area which could be delivered once a week without disrupting other lessons in that subject.

The secondary teacher should ensure that the identified topic is one that will enable their pupils to embed the foundations of their subject. The work is most likely to succeed if whole classes are involved in the collaboration – for example, a secondary maths class is paired with a class in Year 4. The secondary class should spend some time preparing the topic, ensuring that their understanding of the basics are secure, and then in smaller groups designing imaginative ways to work with the primary pupils.

It may be necessary to move to a larger space for the joint lessons if the usual lesson space isn't suitable. The secondary and primary teachers can be on hand to support the event but should resist intervening at the first hiccup. At the end of the session the teachers should find out from their respective pupils how future sessions can be improved and what worked well, and then plan the next lesson accordingly. These weekly events should be mentioned regularly in the 'normal' lessons on this topic, ensuring that both primary and secondary pupils see how their knowledge of the subject is connected and expanding. This initiative should be seen as a regular commitment (for at least a half term), so that relationships are built and the awkwardness of any initial meetings disappears.

This work should not only involve pupils with high ability in the identified subject; it can also be particularly effective for pupils who don't have an obvious natural gift in the area. I have seen a very effective six-month project which involved 15-year-old pupils from lower English sets who worked on a section of literacy with pupils in a local infant school. The project was very popular with pupils on both sides – for many it was a highlight of their week. The infant teacher felt that her pupils were genuinely benefitting from the experience and that their development was progressing faster than she would have expected. Interestingly, the secondary teacher overseeing the work also found that the progress of the secondary pupils in the subject had improved markedly. Both schools had no doubt that the benefits of the work far outweighed any logistical hurdles required to make it happen.

I have also seen very successful projects involving the delivery of units of PE and drama by secondary pupils to primary pupils. I have a vivid memory of watching a Year 4 PE class being led by a group of four 15-year-old boys. This was a regular event, with the primary teacher helping to plan the lessons but then sitting in the wings as an observer during the lesson. The secondary boys were not always fully engaged in their own schoolwork (it would probably be fair to say that they could be quite challenging) yet they behaved in a mature way, and the behaviour of the primary class was exemplary.

If you give pupils the responsibility, they will often surpass your expectations. At its best, this type of project provides benefits not just in terms of pupils' subject learning but also their self-confidence and levels of engagement.

INDUCTION EVENTS

2.1. PASSPORT ACTIVITY

It is important to remember that induction activities are most effective when they follow a long-term transition process. When transition has been well developed, pupils will already feel the connection between the two schools and they will understand that they are on an educational journey. The focus of induction therefore becomes clear: to help pupils understand new ways of being, new people and new places. As a development of the journey metaphor, getting pupils to collect 'stamps' for an induction passport can be a very useful strategy.

OVERVIEW

The whole day is themed around a journey and all the different stages are outlined in a 'passport'. Pupils are given a carousel of activities to complete during the day, and they collect a stamp in their passport for each task they carry out.

DETAILS

This activity should develop out of the school's wider planning for transition, so make a list of all the practical things that you think the pupils need to know about. For example:

- Who the key adults in the school are (matching photos to names).

- How the school refers to the teacher (many secondary schools use staff codes).

- The layout of the school – how to find your way to lessons, the canteen, etc.

- Locations of toilets and the procedures for accessing them.

- The tutor group – what it is and why it exists.

- Other members of the tutor group – their names and where they are from.

- The organisation of the school day.

- What subjects the pupils will be learning.

- The timetable – how it works and how to read one.

- Using the library.

- Procedures for specialist rooms (science, design and technology, art, music, PE, etc.).

- Procedures for paying for lunch/break refreshments.

- Procedures for accessing lunch/break refreshments.

- Procedures for assessing medical support.

- Checking details held by the school (address, emergency contact, medical information, etc.).

- Emergency evacuation procedures.

- Clarifying the uniform rules and specifications.

- Outlining expectations for required stationery.

- Issuing lockers/explaining cloakroom procedures.

I wouldn't recommend that schools deliver all this information in one block. As with any form of learning, the pupils are far more likely to retain the details if they are involved in active methods of learning.

Divide the day into a number of sections – perhaps one for each period of the secondary school day (and in doing so, getting the pupils familiar with the timings of the day). Each group can undertake the activities in a different order to make best use of the resources and the building. Once each section has been successfully completed, the pupil receives a stamp in their passport to signify this. You could include the following activities.

HUNT THE TEACHER

Produce some A5-size cards with the photo of a teacher on one side and some unanswered questions on the back, such as name, staff code, role in the school, tenure at the school, favourite music, favourite film and so on. The pupils can be split into groups of three (ideally with children from different primary schools) and given three cards at random. The group must walk around the school searching for the teachers, and when they find them, ask the questions and note down their answers. It may be helpful for the organising teacher to give some clues as to their location – and, of course, the designated teachers should be on the lookout to help! If a group finishes quickly, they can be given some extra cards to fill in. Once everyone has returned with their completed cards, each group should 'introduce' the teacher on their cards and share the information they have found out. Once completed, all the pupils get a stamp in their passport.

FIND SOMEONE WHO ...

This activity helps pupils in a tutor group to get to know their new classmates. Give each pupil a sheet with the heading: 'Find someone who ...' Ask them to find a pupil who matches the following descriptions:

- Likes pizza.

- Has had a holiday in France.

- Has a famous relative.

- Likes classical music.

- Has been to a gig in the past three months.

- Likes *EastEnders*.

- Thinks there is more happiness than sadness in the world.

- Lives within a kilometre of the school.

- Loves maths.

- Can roll their tongue.

- Has a talent.

- Can draw a cat.

- Would like to go to Hogwarts.

- Has written a poem.

The pupils can only use any name once, and they get a bonus point every time they include the name of someone with whom they didn't go to primary school. Once completed the pupils receive their passport stamp for this activity.

GROUP IDENTITY

This activity might follow on from the 'Find someone who ...' task. As the group are getting to know each other, the focus can move on to how all these individuals will become a group. One way to do this is to produce a group shield or emblem capturing who they are and what they believe. An example could be:

Alternatively, or in addition, the group could complete a large piece of art to represent their group. Each person in the group should be represented and contribute some part of it. When the activity is over the pupils get another passport stamp.

WONDER HUNT

Place some wonder questions on little plaques around the school. Ideas for suitable questions, originating from Independent Thinking's Agent of Wonder Dr Matthew

McFall, can be found in Appendix 3. Show the pupils what the plaques look like and where they can be found (I would recommend placing them in communal areas such as corridors, halls and entrances only). Organise the pupils into small groups (ideally including children from other primaries) and give each group a map of the school site. Allocate a set amount of time for them to go around the school and mark as many wonder questions as they can find on the map (each question should have a unique number). In addition, each group should choose their top three favourite questions. When the groups meet up again, give them a larger group map and get them to identify the location of all the questions. Each group should then present their favourite wonder question and explain why they have selected it. Once they have completed the task they get a wonder stamp in their passport.

SOLVE THE PROBLEM

This activity could be based in the maths department, perhaps taking place across different rooms and involving multiple teachers to enhance the pupils' experience. Set a series of questions with numerical answers which require the pupils to talk to each other (and to the teachers), and then ask them to carry out the mathematical functions.

An example could include:

- How many primary schools are the new pupils from =

- Multiply this by the number of maths teachers in the school =

- Add the number of letters in the surname of the head of maths =

- Divide by the amount of prime numbers between 1 and 100 =

- Add the number of pupils in the new Year 7 =

- Multiply by the number of maths lessons each pupil has each week =

- Minus the cost of a chicken salad sandwich in the canteen =

- Add the number of rooms in the school =

The list can be expanded as much as desired to include a further mix of mathematical and/or personal questions. The final answer should be written in their passport as evidence of the pupil having completed the task.

PRODUCE ARTICLES FOR THE 'TRANSITION TIMES'

One way to celebrate the activities that have been developed between the schools is to ask the pupils to write an article to capture their experiences and what they have learned. To prompt the work, collect a variety of photographs from across the activities (not just the events of the induction days) and ask the pupils in small groups to write copy for a newspaper article to support one of the pictures. Alternatively, one group could write an article about the way the timetable works, another about the meals, another about the head teacher or other staff and so on. They could also include pictures and descriptions of uniform items and where they can be obtained. Pupils from each primary school could also collaborate to write an article describing their own school.

Although completing the activity is the requirement for getting a stamp in their transition passport, schools could be clever and print the newspaper along with some additional information, such as the start time for the first day of term. The newspaper could then be distributed to all parents and primary schools, helping to cement the importance of the transition process in everyone's minds.

MINI PROBLEM-SOLVING ACTIVITY

The problem could be based in an area of science and/or technology and could take the form of a shorter version of any of the ideas suggested in Appendix 1 or the forensic science day (see below). The main objective should be to familiarise the pupils with the science area and to encourage them to work together to solve a problem – for example, using chromatography to work out which pen has been used to write a threatening letter, how to build a bridge to support a weight using only straws and Sellotape, or how to get fresh water from dirty pond water.

2.2. FORENSIC SCIENCE ACTIVITY

Variations on the theme of forensic science have proved to be successful on many transition/induction days. These types of activities provide a fun way to introduce pupils to different areas of the school and the expectations required of pupils when using them.

A popular way to start a forensic science day is to have the pupils 'discover' a murder victim (either a brave teacher or a fake dead body). Many schools go to significant efforts to dress up the murder scene, and some head teachers seem to take much delight in being 'murdered' by a colleague and having the pupils discover who is responsible (usually from a short list of suspicious candidates from within the school staff)! However, a word of caution: please check that no one involved in the transition day has been in a comparable situation in real life. If you have any concerns, a safer form of crime would be a more fun one, such as the theft of the head of science's lunch. Once the scenario has been outlined, the pupils can embark on a variety of sub-activities.

In essence, the forensic science day is an elaborate form of Cluedo, with the board being replaced by the map of the school, the character list by the school staff (either the whole staff body or a suitable shortlist) and the weapons by equipment from the list of school essentials. In this way, the pupils become familiar with elements of the day-to-day life of the school as a by-product of the main activity.

It is helpful to produce A5 cards representing each of the suspects: a photo of the staff member along with their name, role in the school and staff code. Other useful pieces of information could be included, or perhaps there could be blanks for the pupils to research for themselves. Possible locations for the crime (or the suspects) can be marked on a map of the school, with the pupils expected to go to some of these places.

Typically, the pupils then carry out some simple tests to determine who could and could not be involved in the crime. Colour chromatography, plant identification, soil sample testing, hair and fingerprint analysis all provide ways for pupils to use science in an everyday setting.

Other areas of the school can also be included in the activity. For example:

- English: comprehension activities based around witness statements, creative writing tasks for newspapers articles.

- Maths: measurement activities connected to the crime scene, such as density or velocity calculations to rule suspects in or out.

- Humanities: use of sources, reading maps and diagrams, identifying pond/river water.

- PE: movement (e.g. hunting for clues in different parts of the school).

- Art/music/drama: crime scene representations.

- Technology: testing the strength/durability of materials and analysing evidence from the crime scene.

The day's activities can be structured within the usual periods of the school day, enabling the pupils to become familiar with everyday life at the school.

Each group will complete a variety of tasks which are presented to the wider group at the end of the day. The 'investigators' summarise their conclusions about who committed the crime and explain how they have arrived at their decision. The 'culprit' should then be exposed and the correct solution explained.

The pupils should also produce written and photographic evidence of the day, perhaps creating the front page for a fictional newspaper. This newspaper can then be printed and circulated, serving as a reminder of the day and a positive springboard into the life of the new school.

2.3. WONDER AND CURIOSITY DAY

Wonder and curiosity were two of the main drivers of learning in the 16th century, but somehow in our more data-driven times they have become less important to schools. However, under the inspirational watch of Dr Matthew McFall, many schools have recognised the power that they still have to support learning. For this reason, wonder and curiosity provide an ideal focus for an inspirational induction day.

An obvious advantage of a celebration based around wonder is that few schools have discrete wonder lessons or a set wonder curriculum. If an induction day is focused around an established curriculum subject it will need to be delicately balanced to ensure that it fits in with the learning of both phases and is relevant for both primary and secondary pupils. However, when wonder and curiosity are the focus of an induction day, it becomes about the engagement and interest of the pupils, and not about the development of a particular subject.

The first step for this type of theme day is to form a steering group, which should meet up as early as possible. However, with such an important and engaging topic as wonder it might be wise to call them the 'wonder warriors' or 'curiosity club' to help instil an enthusiastic atmosphere and ensure that the right type of people commit to it. The induction day shouldn't be the only item on the agenda at their first meeting. They should also be encouraged to develop their own curiosity and excitement in learning before trying to inspire this in the pupils.

I recall a particularly effective session where Matthew McFall hosted a trip of key people from each of the primary and secondary schools serving Ramsey, on the Isle of Man, at a very large junk shop, where each person was given £5 and 30 minutes to buy an item that fed their own curiosity. They then had to share their objects with the rest of the group and find ways to use it in their work. The key point here is that the organisers need to be enthusiastic and not approach this as just another task to be completed.

Once the group has been established give them the power to plan a high-energy and engaging day. As with previous activities, if the group requires a convenor or leader I would recommend that this should not naturally be one of the secondary school representatives. Wonder should have no hierarchy. However, you do need to be clear with the group about what else you would like pupils to gain from the day (e.g. staff names, room locations, procedures for lunch/break, uniform regulations, timings of the day). These can be imaginatively built in to the main themes of the day.[1]

It can be beneficial to have several different wonder-themed activities which smaller groups of pupils can rotate between. Here are some suggestions.

WONDER ROOM

A wonder room is a specialist room which can be a permanent installation or a temporary one constructed specially for the day. I have seen both work very well, although I would advise that if you create a temporary room that you construct it using reusable boards. The wonder room should contain a mass of interesting objects; collecting them together may well be one of the tasks of the steering group.

Examples of objects that might be included are old keys, skeletons, puzzles (wooden/metal/plastic), seeds, insects, typewriters, old phones, unusual plants, 3D images, old drawings, optical illusions (2D and 3D), unusual materials, props from old movies, fossils, unusual rocks, interesting science equipment (Galileo thermometer, Van de Graaff generator, etc.), old coins, old farming tools, items relevant

---

1 An interesting aside: adding restrictions often increases creativity rather than decreases it – see Phil Beadle's *Dancing About Architecture: A Little Book of Creativity* (Independent Thinking Series) (Carmarthen: Crown House Publishing, 2011) for more on this.

to local history, optical equipment, astronomical apparatus and so on. The items should be displayed in an imaginative way, with labelling when needed, and suitable questions to prompt interaction.

Each group can be given a set time to investigate the room. They must then choose their three favourite items and explain their reasoning to the rest of the group. The final part of the task could take place away from the wonder room if necessary. An extension of this activity could be for the group to plan a tour of the room by a special guest (e.g. senior leader, parent, pupil from a different age group), during which five items would be shown and explained to them.

WONDER HUNT

Place some wonder questions on little plaques around the school. Possible questions can be found in Appendix 3. Show the pupils what the plaques look like and where they can be found (I would recommend placing them in communal areas such as corridors, halls and entrances only). Organise the pupils into small groups (ideally including children from other primaries) and give each group a map of the school site. Allocate a set amount of time for them to go around the school and mark as many wonder questions as they can on the map (each question should have a unique number). In addition, each group should choose their top three favourite questions. When the groups meet up again, give them a larger group map and ask them to identify the location of all the questions. Each group should then present their favourite wonder question and explain why they have selected it.

WONDER LESSON

Give the pupils a box (or similar) containing a collection of objects from the wonder room – around 10 to 15 objects works well. In groups of four or five (ideally containing a mix of pupils from each primary school) the children should choose one item on which to focus. They must then plan how they would use the item to introduce a lesson in the main curriculum (e.g. using a honeycomb as part of a maths lesson). They should identify what learning it will help with and then design a five-minute session to do this. The lesson can either be 'taught' to the remainder of the group, to an invited teacher or to a selected group of older pupils.

WONDER MAP

Each group involved in the induction day should be given a map showing the secondary school, its grounds and parts of the local community. The group should visit as much of the area depicted as possible. As they are doing so, they should search for items that make them curious, such as a very old tree, a strange-shaped roof or an old phone box that has been repurposed to contain a defibrillator. They should then find ways to represent these objects on a wonder map which can be copied for wider distribution. The benefits of implying that learning and wonder go together, and that the community contains plenty of things to be curious about, are numerous.

WONDER INVESTIGATION

The teacher selects an object of wonder for the children to investigate. The pupils are given the object to feel and consider, and then in groups they ask questions about the object: what does it do? Why? How did it come to exist? What happens if ...? The most effective items will produce questions which the pupils can carry out experiments to find out the answer – for example, can you fold a piece of paper in half more than nine times? How high can the contents of a bottle of pop travel if it has a sugar mint placed in it? What is the biggest bubble that can be produced? How many pins can be put in an inflated balloon without it bursting? What is the maximum number of dominos that can be set up (and then knocked down) in 30 minutes? This is all about increasing pupil engagement, and it works best when the pupils are driving the questions.

COMMUNITY CURIOSITY EVENT

Ask the pupils in groups to plan an afterschool (or Saturday) event to which the wider community (parents, local business people and so on) can be invited. The pupils should spend 30 minutes in the wonder room finding the items that most interest them. They should then share their thoughts as a group, and between them select 30–40 items that they think visitors from the community might be interested in. They should select objects that will interest adults and children both younger and older than themselves.

Once they have chosen the items, they should take them to the room/area where the event will occur and decide how to display them. The pupils can then produce signs and leaflets about the objects. They should also think about writing instructions for the pupils who will host the event. These can include more detailed information about the items (e.g. history and use) as well as instructions on how the pupils should greet their guests and practical arrangements such as refreshments and toilets. Advertising the event in the community could be an additional task, and would ensure that a full range of skills are developed by the pupils involved.

2.4. ARTS-BASED DAY

The first step in planning an arts-based day is to form a group containing the teachers responsible for the art/drama/music/textiles/dance in each of the schools. Initially, it is important not to overwhelm the group with all the induction hopes and demands that you may have for the day. Instead, encourage the group to focus on what makes them most passionate, which is likely to be the arts and the pupils' development in them.

A good early exercise for the group would be for each teacher to bring in examples of pupils' artwork that fills them with hope, pride and happiness. From this initial sharing of potential, the task for the group should be to find a theme within the arts which they believe would:

● Motivate large numbers of pupils (and staff).

● Bring out the variety of talents in the schools (not just those of the singers and painters).

● Encourage versatility (so the day doesn't celebrate 400 versions of the same piece of art).

This could take the form of a broad title such as Happiness, Strength, Learning, Family, Inspiration or Curiosity, or a more precise topic such as Isaac Newton, Birmingham, Artificial Intelligence or The Year 2000.

Once the theme has been decided, each school should dedicate a period of time within the arts curriculum to focus on this topic. This should not just involve Year 6 pupils, but preferably secondary groups and other primary years too. As many examples of 2D and 3D artwork as possible should be gathered together in the secondary school (this will be the location for the induction activity) and an impressive display made in advance of the transition day.

On the induction day itself, groups of pupils should spend time visiting the exhibition and choosing their favourite artworks. Some groups will 'curate' the visit for other pupils or even prepare visits for their parents or teachers later in the day: they will decide what is included in the exhibition, how people view it and answer any questions from visitors. There should also be opportunities during the day to share performance work, such as dance and drama pieces, with a wider audience. Other pupils not participating in these events could be given the role of journalist and should try to capture what they have seen in words and photographs.

A high point of the day could be to commission an experienced 3D/large-scale artist who would be tasked to work with groups of pupils to produce a large piece of art (or pieces – one for each primary school) to represent the chosen theme. This can give pupils new skills and experiences while also providing a permanent reminder of the work they complete together. This could be a sculpture made from recycled items, a collage of pupil work or even a website. (One of my favourites was a gigantic mural where every pupil and member of staff cut, shaped, painted and glazed their own 1cm cube of clay, which were then formed into an artwork in the school entrance.)

Of course, whatever aspect of the arts the pupils have been immersed in, the secondary school will also want to ensure that new pupils learn the names of at least some staff members and get to know about the school's routines, room numbers, layout, arrangements for lunch, the rhythms and rules of the building and so on. Fundamentals like this can be absorbed by the pupils as part of their induction day, rather than be the focus of it. It is quite likely that they will remember much more of the information gained in this way.

Following the induction day, the materials produced – including accounts and photos by the pupils involved – will form an excellent advertisement for the positive relationship between the schools. A display can be made which can tour primary schools, local supermarkets, village halls or libraries.

2.5. THEME-BASED DAY

This is a project for a group of schools which feel they have a robust transition programme in place, have been working together across the ages in a variety of ways and want the special induction day to be a celebration of that relationship. Something more akin to the opening ceremony of a big event rather than a day steeped in the practicalities of learning new procedures.

The theme chosen can be almost anything – for example:

- An area of the world (e.g. the venue for a World Cup or Olympic Games).

- A local town, village or building.

- A specific year (e.g. a significant local date).

- A person from history (e.g. a local inventor).

- An industry or profession (e.g. aviation if the school is near an airport).

- A particular subject (e.g. literacy, if this is an area-wide priority).

- A philosophical question (see Ian Gilbert's *Compleat Book of Thunks* – e.g. 'Is there more future than past?' 'It is OK to bully a bully?'[2]).

Once the theme has been chosen, a steering group should be formed including a range of teachers across all the schools. The group should identify ways in which different curriculum areas could feed into the selected theme. Subject areas in the secondary school should then start to design activities for inclusion in the special day. In addition, local experts, musicians, artists and speakers could be approached to add an extra dimension to the event. This should lead to a carousel of activities for the pupils to experience.

Traditional induction activities (issuing lockers, learning about the timetable, etc.) can be covered subtly during the themed day, delivered in prior events or left until the start of the term, with any essentials addressed in a letter prior to the start of term. It is important that this type of event can stand in isolation and be a thoroughly enjoyable and memorable day, which just happens to mark the pupils' move to secondary school.

The day should be captured on video, in audio recordings, photographs and pupil reports, and then shared widely across the community. Where possible, make permanent displays in libraries, shops and all the participating schools. This will celebrate the topic being studied as well as the way the schools work together.

---

2 I. Gilbert, *The Compleat Thunks Book* (Carmarthen: Independent Thinking Press, 2017).

WONDER QUESTIONS

Here are some riddles, Thunks, trick questions, meaningful questions, paradoxes, celebrations and jokes which have been collected together by Agent of Wonder Dr Matthew McFall:

1   Who are you?

2   If you had to change your name what would you call yourself?

3   Where are you from?

4   What is your favourite colour?

5   What do you want to be?

6   What is your favourite animal?

7   What is your earliest memory?

8   Who inspires you?

9   When did you begin?

10 What are you optimistic about?

11 How would you describe yourself in three words?

12 How do you know that you are alive?

13 What is your lucky number?

14 What is your happiest memory?

15 What is your favourite song?

16   What would you like to change about the world?

17   Do you dream in colour?

18   What is your favourite place in the world?

19   What is your favourite food?

20   What are you most grateful for?

21   What is the best book you've ever read?

22   What does wonder mean to you?

23   Who do you love?

24   What is an anagram?

25   How old do you feel?

26   What can you hear?

27   Where will you be in ten years' time?

28   Why did the chicken cross the road?

29   What has a tongue but cannot speak?

30   What is a palindrome?

31   What is the hardest question to answer?

32   To which question must you always answer yes?

33   What three misteaks can you find in this question

34   What's in the box?

35   What do you call people born in Nottinghamshire?

36   What is special about the number 8549176320?

37   What is the difference between a maze and a labyrinth?

38   What time is it?

39 How can a person become wise?

40 What is the most random thing in the universe?

41 Where can peace be found?

42 Why are some people superstitious?

43 Would you like to travel forwards or backwards in time?

44 Why are some people scared of the dark?

45 How can a person make a difference?

46 How many senses do you have?

47 What is the most dangerous thing in the world?

48 Is there life on other planets?

49 What is wrong with this this question?

50 Is this a poem?

51 What is the meaning of life?

52 What is the best thing in the world?

53 What makes the world go round?

54 What is love?

55 How many beans make five?

56 Do fish drink?

57 Can a snail smell?

58 How many toes does a cat have?

59 Why is water wet?

60 What happens if you press the button?

61 Why are rainbows curved?

62 What is normal?

63 How do magnets work?

64 What is gravity?

65 How is the human race evolving?

66 What is the most important invention in history?

67 How many hairs are there on your head?

68 Is the universe friendly or unfriendly?

69 What is the biggest number?

70 When you eat an egg are you eating a bird?

71 Is a computer clever?

72 Can a baby commit a crime?

73 Why are you here?

74 What special power would you most like to develop?

75 What advice would you give to your younger self?

76 What is never odd or even?

77 I have a bee in my hand. What do I have in my eye?

78 What is the sound of one hand clapping?

79 How does Monday differ from every other day of the week?

80 Name three vegetables that begin with the letter 'T'.

81 What's orange and sounds like a parrot?

82 What has an inside but no outside?

83 What came first: the chicken or the egg?

84 What is the most boring thing in the universe?

85 How old is (name of your community)?

86 How many legs does an insect have?

87 When did the world begin?

88 How do mirrors work?

89 What is electricity?

90 Is there life on other planets?

91 What is magic?

92 What's your favourite word?

93 Is it ever possible to learn nothing?

94 What's the secret of happiness?

95 What colour are brains?

96 Who invented forks?

97 Are dinosaurs still alive?

98 Which city is furthest from (your community)?

99 How many languages have been spoken on Earth?

100 What's your favourite question?

REFERENCES AND FURTHER READING

Beadle, P. (2011) *Dancing About Architecture: A Little Book of Creativity* (Independent Thinking Series) (Carmarthen: Crown House Publishing).

Borman, G. D., Rozek, C. S., Pyne, J. and Hanselman, P. (2019) Reappraising Academic and Social Adversity Improves Middle School Students' Academic Achievement, Behavior, and Well-Being, *Proceedings of the National Academy of Sciences of the United States of America* 116(33): 16286–16291.

Briggs, S. (2013) How Peer Teaching Improves Student Learning and 10 Ways to Encourage It, *informED* (7 June). Available at: https://www.opencolleges.edu.au/informed/features/peer-teaching.

Curran, A. (2008) *The Little Book of Big Stuff About the Brain: The True Story of Your Amazing Brain* (Independent Thinking Series) (Carmarthen: Crown House Publishing).

Evangelou, M., Taggart, B., Sylva, K., Melhuish, E., Sammons, P. and Siraj-Blatchford, I. (2008) *What Makes a Successful Transition from Primary to Secondary School?* Research Report DCSF-RR019 (London: Department for Children, Schools and Families). Available at: https://dera.ioe.ac.uk/8618/1/DCSF-RR019.pdf.

Gilbert, I. (2017) *The Compleat Thunks Book* (Carmarthen: Independent Thinking Press).

Haapala, E. A., Haapala, H. L., Syväoja, H., Tammelin, T. H., Finni, T. and Kiuru, N. (2019) Longitudinal Associations of Physical Activity and Pubertal Development with Academic Achievement in Adolescents, *Journal of Sport and Health Science*. https://doi.org/10.1016/j.jshs.2019.07.003.

Hanewald, R. (2013) Transition Between Primary and Secondary School: Why It Is Important and How It Can Be Supported, *Australian Journal of Teacher Education* 38(1): 62–74.

Harris, D. (2007) *Are You Dropping the Baton? From Effective Collaboration to All-Through Schools – Your Guide to Improving Transition* (Independent Thinking Series) (Carmarthen: Crown House Publishing).

Harris, D. and West-Burnham, J. (2018) *Leadership Dialogues II: Leadership in Times of Change* (Carmarthen: Crown House Publishing).

Jindal-Snape, D., Cantali, D., MacGillivray, S. and Hannah, E. (2019) *Primary to Secondary School Transitions: Systematic Literature Review* (Edinburgh: Scottish Government). Available at: https://www.gov.scot/publications/primary-secondary-transitions-systematic-literature-review/pages/2.

King, Jr., M. L. (1992 [1947]) The Purpose of Education. In C. Carson, R. Luker and P. A. Russell (eds), *The Papers of Martin Luther King, Jr. Vol. I: Called to Serve, January 1929–June 1951* (Berkeley, CA: University of California Press), pp. 123–124.

Lee, H. (1989 [1960]) *To Kill a Mockingbird* (London: Arrow).

McFall, M. (2013) *The Little Book of Awe and Wonder: A Cabinet of Curiosities* (Carmarthen: Independent Thinking Press).

McLellan, R. and Galton, M. (2015) *The Impact of Primary–Secondary Transition on Students' Wellbeing* (Cambridge: University of Cambridge and Nuffield Foundation). Available at: https://www.educ.cam.ac.uk/people/staff/mclellan/Final-Report-June-2015.pdf.

Maslow, A. H. (1954) *Motivation and Personality* (New York: Harper & Row).

Morrison, I., Everton, T., Rudduck, J., Cannie, J. and Strommen, L. (2000) Pupils Helping Other Pupils with Their Learning: Cross-Age Tutoring in a Primary and Secondary School, *Mentoring & Tutoring* 8(3): 190–197.

National Centre for Excellence in the Teaching of Maths (2019) Why We Employed a Primary Teacher for Maths in Our Secondary School (11 April). Available at: https://www.ncetm.org.uk/resources/53069.

Nicholson, N. (1987) The Transition Cycle: A Conceptual Framework for the Analysis of Change and Human Resource

Management, *Research in Personnel and Human Resources Management* 5: 167–222.

Rice, F., Frederickson, N., Shelton, K., McManus, C., Riglin, L. and Ng-Knight, T. (2008) *Identifying Factors That Predict Successful and Difficult Transitions to Secondary School*. Available at: https://www.nuffieldfoundation.org/sites/default/files/files/STARS_report.pdf.

Stobart, A. (2016) *Transition Toolkit: Helping You Support a Child Through Change* (London: Autism Education Trust). Available at: http://www.learningsupportcentre.com/wp-content/uploads/2016/01/Autism-Education-Trust-Transition-Toolkit.pdf.

Tobbell, J. (2014) Transition from Primary to Secondary School: A Case Study from the United Kingdom. In A. B. Liegmann, I. Mammes and K. Racherbäumer (eds), *Facetten von Übergängen im Bildungssystem: Nationale und internationale Ergebnisse empirischer Forschung* (Münster: Waxmann), pp. 251–264.

University of Wisconsin-Madison (2019) Power of Refocusing Student Stress in Middle School Transition: Sixth Graders Taught to See Transition Turmoil as 'Normal, Temporary' Perform Better in Class, *Science Daily* (29 July). Available at: https://www.sciencedaily.com/releases/2019/07/190729164630.htm.

van Rens, M., Haelermans, C., Groot, W. and Maassen van den Brink, H. (2018) Facilitating a Successful Transition to Secondary School: (How) Does it Work? A Systematic Literature Review, *Adolescent Research Review* 3(1): 43–56. Available at: https://link.springer.com/article/10.1007%2Fs40894-017-0063-2.

Vaz, S., Falkmer, M., Ciccarelli, M. and Passmore, A. E. (2015) Belongingness in Early Secondary School: Key Factors that Primary and Secondary Schools Need to Consider, *PLoS ONE* 10(9): e0136053.

West-Burnham, J. and Harris, D. (2014) *Leadership Dialogues: Conversations and Activities for Leadership Teams* (Carmarthen: Crown House Publishing).